THE OLDEST POST OFFICE IN THE WORLD

AND OTHER SCOTTISH ODDITIES

HAMISH BROWN

SANDSTONEPRESS
HIGHLAND | SCOTLAND

First published in Great Britain by
Sandstone Press Ltd
PO Box 5725
One High Street
Dingwall
Ross-shire
IV15 9WJ
Scotland.

www.sandstonepress.com

Editor: Robert Davidson
Maps: David Langworth, Melrose
Scans from Hamish Brown's original slides: David Ritchie, Dingwall

The publisher acknowledges subsidy from Creative Scotland towards publication of this volume.

ISBN: 978-1-905207-95-4

Other Hamish Brown titles published by Sandstone Press include:
Hamish's Mountain Walk
Hamish's Groats End Walk

Book design and typeset by Raspberryhmac Graphic Design, Edinburgh.
Printed and bound in the EU.

INTRODUCTION

We do have quite a number of the curious, weird, surprising and unconventional, the range which is covered by *Oddities*. To me, one Scottish characteristic is a marked sense of the ridiculous. A plethora of oddities is not surprising. Purely natural phenomena such as caves, waterfalls, fossils, etc, have been omitted (someone is welcome to compile a companion volume!), and the selection kept to the works and inspiration of human heads, hearts and hands. The few seemingly natural oddities owe their inclusion to human manipulation.

I have visited every site included in what is a very personal choice as I do dislike describing anything other than from personal experience, beside which I wanted to have an illustration if possible. Other nearby interests or the opportunity to enjoy a local walk may also be mentioned briefly. Reference books and the internet can be surprisingly inaccurate with information, with basic facts wrong and dates doubtful. I apologise for errors, but reject the blame. And isn't part of the fun and the very making of an Oddity due to the idiosyncratic nature of humankind?

Two volumes are envisioned in order to keep a topical and geographical spread. For instance, the Italian chapel in Orkney is well known but I was thrilled to discover a comparable story in the revamped Kelvingrove, so at once there is a story for each volume – as there is for Edinburgh and Glasgow 'walkabouts', something about Covenanters, bell towers, clocks, bus stops, bridges or whalebone arches.

Recycling appears: a church turned into a garage, a water tower as an art gallery, a lighthouse as a hotel … Someone sent me a couple of foreign names appearing on our maps (Moscow, Portobello) suggesting there might be others. Indeed there are; my list runs from Abyssinia via Joppa, Patna and Troy to Zanzibar. And then there is the fact that Edinburgh lies further west than Liverpool … And what about the gates to Edinburgh Univesity's Old Quad being erected to keep out the police? An 1838 town v students snowball fight got a bit out of hand; after two days the Riot Act was read and the police went in. The university authorities took a dim view of this so had the gates erected. There's something of trivial pursuits in these volumes.

I have divided Scotland into 13 areas, shown on an introductory map while each feature has a map showing its location and, usually, a six figure reference, given with the Ordnance Survey Land Ranger 1: 50,000 map sheet number, e.g.: OS 76: 022995.

While this is an excellent book for dipping into or for bedside reading it is also a guide book so should perhaps be kept in the car. Better still, buy two: one for the home, one for away! They will become well-thumbed I hope, both at home and in roaming this extraordinary country of Scotland.

Hamish Brown
Burntisland 2012
(which is not an island,
has never been burned,
and is not called Burntis-land.)

MAP OF SCOTLAND (showing divisions used)

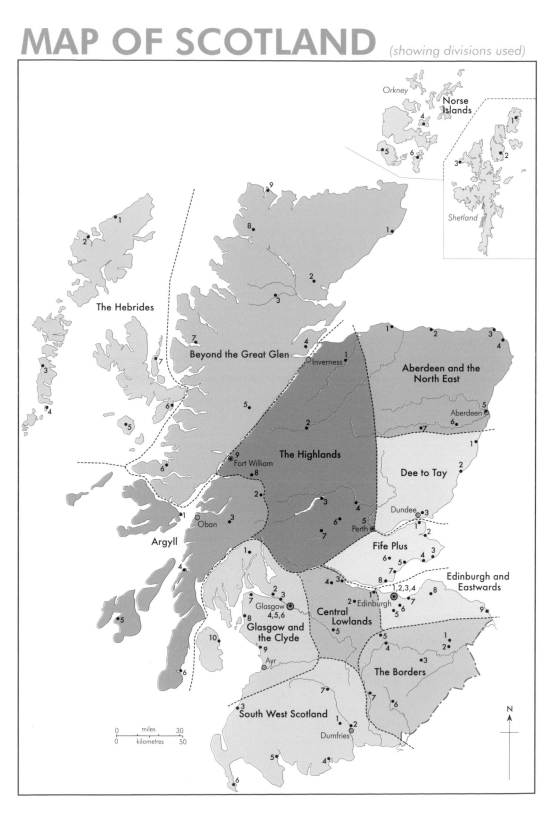

Orkney

Norse Islands

Shetland

The Hebrides

Beyond the Great Glen

Inverness

Aberdeen and the North East

Aberdeen

The Highlands

Fort William

Dee to Tay

Dundee

Argyll

Oban

Perth

Fife Plus

Edinburgh and Eastwards

Glasgow

Central Lowlands

Edinburgh

Glasgow and the Clyde

Ayr

The Borders

South West Scotland

Dumfries

0 miles 30
0 kilometres 50

N

CONTENTS

Shetland Islands Council

BUS STOP IN UNST

This is the most delightful oddity in this book and brings Shetland visitors from miles away to see it; though barely mentioned officially, everyone just talks about it, the best recommendation of all. Years ago a schoolboy waiting for his bus in this glass box in the middle of nowhere took a chair over to wait more comfortably. Then he took something else and something else.

In August 2007 when I last saw the bus stop a note declared, 'This year's colour is yellow'. And so it was: all the walls draped in canary bright curtains, armchair and couch covered in yellow, a table with TV and computer, side table with kettle and tea-making necessities, van Gogh's *Sunflowers* on the wall, a vase of marigolds. No wonder it drew the visitors and no other oddity draws such smiles.

The bus stop is on Unst, the most northerly Shetland isle (OS Sheet 1), near the natural curiosity of the Keen of Hamar, on the A968 between Baltasound (with the most northerly PO) and Haroldswick (with the 'Boat Haven' the most northerly museum). The only sad note was how often I heard people say that such a delightful piece of fun wouldn't last twenty-four hours where they lived, but then Shetland was so far from anywhere. This last comment does not go down well. Shetland is not far from Shetland. On a previous visit I brought back a tea towel displaying a map of Shetland and, in the top corner, an inset showing the rest of the British Isles.

OS1: 636097

WHITE WIFE, QUEYON

It is hard to imagine just how dangerous travel by ship must have been back in the days of sailing vessels. Yell, Shetland, has a monument to one tragedy inconceivable today in the form of the figurehead from a ship, which was erected in sight of the spot where she was wrecked.

The figurehead shows a female in flowing dress, left hand holding some folds, right hand clasping a book to her breast, the Bible presumably, all white but for book and belt and golden yellow hair. The story behind this odd memorial?

She was from a Hamburg owned ship, the *Bohus*, a 1487 ton barque, built of iron in 1892 at Alloa on the upper Forth and, besides trading, was used as a training ship for the German Navy.

In April 1924 *Bohus* sailed from Gothenburg, Sweden, during a period of bad spring storms, bound for Taltal, Chile, with 250 tons of sand in ballast. No chance of a sighting on the sun was possible and she sailed 'by guess and by God' as they say. When land was eventually glimpsed the captain guessed this was Fair Isle so set course to have it pass on the port side. The land, however, was Out Skerries 60 miles further north.

Visibility was poor (less than a mile) and they were running before a SE gale. Horrors then to observe land some hours later off both port and starboard bows – Yell and Fetlar. The ship would not come round, an anchor was dropped but with 25 fathoms run out, the cable broke, and she was helpless on the lee shore of the Ness of Queyon. Some crew leapt overboard on grounding, most slid into the water when she fell to seaward, all had to swim for their lives and, with 49 aboard (16 crew, 22 cadets, 1 stowaway) it was regarded as near miraculous that only four perished. Two lie in Mid Yell kirkyard and one, the cook, took off after gaining land and was never seen again. Twenty minutes after striking, *Bohus* went down. Several ships were wrecked on Shetland during this period.

The figurehead later drifted ashore and was set up as a monument to the tragedy. A replica of the figurehead can be seen in the Old Haa at Burravoe (SE corner of Yell). Shetland Amenity Trust have restored the figurehead more recently so, there, she stands, the White Lady, White Wife, or, more colloquially, the Widden Wife.

Yell is the first island north of the Shetland Mainland, connected by vehicle ferry, Toft to Ulsta. From Ulsta the B9081 circles the SE coast, passing Burravoe, Otterswick and Mid Yell before joining the A968 which circles up the SW coast. Near Otterswick Queyon and 'White Wife' are signposted. There's a car park just before the road-end farm and the path to the figurehead indicated. The site is oddly indicated by 'stone' on the map.

OS 2: 529854

3

A STUPID KILLER

One could feel a bit sorry for Laurence Tulloch. Having his name and 'stupidity' carved in stone for generations to see is a bit hard. He didn't mean to kill Donald Robertson whose own description is slightly ambiguous.

Esha Ness is one of the most spectacular corners of mainland Shetland, with great cliff scenery, rising to over 50m at the Stevenson lighthouse. (Rocks on the ground have been tossed there by winter storms!) Down in the lee of this exposed headland is a small graveyard (Cross Kirk) which has one of the oddest of gravestone inscriptions: 'Donald Robertson, b.1785 d.1848 aged 63 years. He was a peaceable, quiet man and to all appearances a quiet Christian. His death was very much regretted which was caused by the stupidity of Laurence Tulloch in Clothister who sold him nitrate instead of Epsom Salts by which he was killed in the space of five hours after taking a dose of it'. Tulloch flitted to Aberdeen and opened a shop there in 1852.

The B9078 through Esha Ness is left to follow the smaller road up to the lighthouse. Just past a loch, on the left, a small track leads to the graveyard. Look for a table stone in the middle. The writing is clear.

OS 3: 212780

4
THE DOUCHE

Shapinsay is separated from Mainland Orkney by a narrow channel called The String and is reached by a 25 minute ferry crossing from Kirkwall. The landing is at the pretty village of Balfour. The tower of the Douche (Dishan Tower) will be spotted nearing the island – as will the Victorian extravaganza of Balfour Castle.

The Douche is the small crenellated tower on the shore with an odd crow-stepped addition on top. It was built as a saltwater shower and the top part is a doocot (dovecote) or it was a doocot first, then shower – reference books do not agree – but it is certainly odd. Equally unusual is the tidal loo at the harbour (two rooms; doubles). Most books only mention Isle Ornsay (Skye) as having such a feature (see p41). From the pierhead walk towards the obvious bulky gatehouse and through a gap to the right of it. Turn left through a gate into a field with the Douche obvious.

The Balfour fortunes were made in India in the C18, the castle was completed in 1848 (David Bryce the architect) and the laird also built the village and revived agriculture after the kelp industry collapsed. Something of a tyrant he at least didn't clear the people as happened on Rousay and elsewhere. After World War Two the estate was bought by one Tadeus Zawadski an officer in the Polish Lancers who had escaped the Katyn massacre.

Ferry: Orkney Isles Shipping Co, several sailings daily (tel: 01856-872044). The castle is sometimes open for public tours, check with the TIC in Kirkwall (tel: 01856-872856).

OS 6: 478162

DWARFIE STANE

Sir Walter Scott toured Orkney and Shetland and elsewhere with the Commissioners of the Northern Lights in 1814, not long after the anonymously-written *Waverley* had appeared. Never one to waste 'copy', out of this voyage would come *The Pirate* (see below). He climbed Sumburgh Head, saw Mousa broch and visited the Dwarfie Stane – which he incorporated in his novel. His authorship of the novels only became clear in 1827 but I wonder if some commissioners didn't have an idea of who was responsible.

This great sandstone slab (roughly 28x14ft / 8.5x4.2m) probably fell from the cliffs higher up on the south slope of a valley which runs across Hoy near Ward Hill, 1570ft/479m, Orkney's highest hill. In the west face of the embedded stone an opening was made which runs in as a passage for about 7½ft/2m and, off this, on each side, a cell has been cut out. A separate block outside looks as if intended to seal the entrance. The plan is the same as for Maes Howe and led to it being recognised as the 'first and only' rock-cut Neolithic/Early Bronze Age tomb in Britain. (One has subsequently been recognised at Glendalough in Ireland.)

From the ferry landing at Moaness there's a walk of an hour to reach the Dwarfie Stane. There's a car park on this minor road for Rackwick and the site lies half a kilometre up under the crags of the Dwarfie Hamars – which end at the Trowie (Trolls) Glen.

The real 'Pirate' was Orcadian John Gow, who went to sea as a youth and, later, made several attempts to seize ships before finally succeeding. On the way back from the Barbary Coast (cargo of beeswax) the officers were murdered and he turned pirate (so mentioned by Defoe in 1724). In 1725 he raided Orkney but on a shore raid some of his men escaped, word was out, and everything went wrong for him. He was captured, taken to London and hanged, twice (the rope had broken after four minutes the first time).

A folly in Kirkwall's Bridge Street has a spire constructed from the volcanic ballast of Gow's ship.

OS 7: 243004

6

HORSING ABOUT IN SOUTH RONALDSAY

St Margaret's Hope (St Margaret's *haven*, old Norse – and appropriate) is an attractive, quiet village on South Ronaldsay, the most southerly of the islands linked by the Churchill Barriers and the most southerly of Orkney's seventy islands. At one time a busy herring port with an agricultural background the island today commemorates its agricultural past with an odd ceremony, the Festival of the Horse which includes a Boys' Ploughing Match.

This began in the middle of the C19, a spin-off from the more serious adult ploughing competitions. The huge Clydesdales would be enthusiastically groomed and decorated by the ploughmen. Boys, as boys do, imitated their fathers and made miniature ploughs then, after World War One, a blacksmith began making more accurate miniatures, treasured and passed down in local families. Like most of our fun doings the competition among the boys is taken with serious dedication – down on the nearby Sands o' Wright, fathers standing by giving advice, the children showing admirable control and skill.

Previous to this the girls had had their showing off at the Hope Community School. The Clydesdales have gone but their memory lingers in local girls being dressed-up in a now traditional style to represent the horses: over their variously decorated black costumes wearing harnesses, blinkers, tails, with cuffs and ankles with white ruffs in imitation of the feathery feet of the Clydesdales. They are competitive too, with categories for best harness and best decoration. Like many old traditions there has been a growing enthusiasm over recent years. A piper led out thirteen ploughboys and fifteen horses when I saw the event in 2010. They were lined up in front of a large audience. And a keen wind and splattering showers didn't disrupt the ploughing match later, contested by serious older lads down to parent-assisted wobbly three year olds.

The festival takes place on the third Saturday in August (13.30 and 15.00). Pentland Ferries operate a speedy vehicle service from Gills Bay (near John o' Groats) to St Margaret's Hope (tel: 01856-831226) and there's also a summer passenger-only John o' Groats – Burwick ferry (tel: 01955-611353). Nearby is one of the interesting prehistoric interpretive sites *The Tomb of the Eagles* (tel: 01856-831339).

OS 7: 448935

WHALIGOE STEPS

A tiny harbour on the cliff-girt coast south of Wick in Caithness can only be reached by a dizzy cliff-held flight of steps (330 or 365 of them deciding who is believed). These zigzag between rock cliffs and serve a flat area in the geo (cliff inlet) called the Bink where ships brought in their catches. The fish was carried up all those steps on the backs of men and women to the fish-curing station on top. The steps were created by estate owner Captain David Brodie in 1788 and cost £8. In 1808 seven boats were based here, in 1814 double that, and by 1826 twenty four worked out of the tiny harbour. In severe weather the boats were actually dragged up the cliffs by a system of pulleys to keep them out of reach of the waves. Caithness was the most important herring fishery in Europe. There were 'silver darlings' indeed but what desperate struggle went to gain the harvest. Telford, surveying the coast, thought it 'a dreadful (i.e. fearsome) place'.

The steps went into decay, with landslides blocking access and destroying steps but were rescued, almost single-handedly by a local lady Mrs Etta Juhle who cared for this assiduously for several decades. They are still cared for by dedicated, unofficial, locals. About 10km south from Wick or 8km north of Lybster there is a signpost pointing *inland* for the ancient site of Cairn of Get. On the *opposite* side of the A9 take the road along past the row of cottages to a car park. The large building to seaward is the old curing station. Skirt it to the start of the steps. Take great care and remember every step in descent is going to be one taken in ascent; not for the unfit or faint-hearted. In a box at the start of the visit or elsewhere you may find a booklet by Iain Sutherland on sale which fully describes the Whaligoe story. Do buy one: the money goes for the upkeep of this priceless piece of our heritage or you may meet Davie Nicolson who lives in one of the cottages and is happy to enthuse about the site, odd only in the sense of being truly extraordinary.

OS12: 321404

2

FIRST CLASS SLEEPERS
AT ROGART

A first-class compartment without the shuggling can be enjoyed at Rogart, a small station on the Wick/Thurso line north of Dingwall. Almost two decades ago railway enthusiasts Kate and Frank Roach created this idyllic rural accommodation for intrigued travellers. There are three carriages (in their Rogart livery) which came on low-loaders from Swindon, Crewe and Duffton. You can imagine the fun lifting them into place; probably the most exciting event in Rogart since Mary Queen of Scots didn't pass through. (She went off the rails.)

Each carriage has shower, toilet, three sleeper compartments, diner and kitchen, thoroughly modern and comfy but still distinctly 'railway'. For railway enthusiasts there is also the fun of being at a real station with real traffic going by. The up passenger may wait a few minutes while a long 'pipe train' goes through. (Pipes for the construction yard near Wick where they are welded together and towed out to the rigs.) There's a working shunter engine, a 1950s Ruston which came from the Tyne docks and an old RAF bus now in the livery of Sutherland Transport.

The setting is delightfully peaceful, a rural idyll, flowery on these platforms, tomatoes and peppers in the smart signal box, timber stack and a pile of wooden sleepers. The visitor book is full of excursions done from Rogart *by train* and many entries are from families making repeat visits. Rogart Station is at Pittentrail on the A839 between the Mound on theA9 and Lairg. Turn down to the station at the war memorial. Sleeperzzz.com. Tel: 01408 641343.

A last little touch. Your receipt is a dated and punched old-fashioned train ticket.

OS 16: 724019

3

THE SHAME OF CROIK

The visitor feels Croick is a long way away from anywhere which makes what one discovers even more poignant. From Ardgay on the A9 (south of Bonar Bridge on the Kyle of Sutherland) take the minor road signposted for Croick, etc and simply follow the road into the hills for about 17km. Croik (1827) was one of over 30 Highland churches and manses designed by Thomas Telford who was glad to take on the commission to help the often poor rural people. He would have been appalled at what was to happen at Croik. The interior is little altered with the original pulpit and long communion table, an atmospheric place.

Stories about the Highland Clearances are usually rather grim but few are remembered as well as here. Four to five hundred people lived in the glen, the estates of Greenyards and Glen Calvie. Glen Calvie paid their rents and lived quietly where the glens met yet they were suddenly told to leave their ancestral homes. The land was wanted for more profitable sheep. When the crunch finally came almost eighty people made their way to the church and made what shelter they could, cowering in the kirkyard. The church was closed: ministers were placed by the landowners after all and preached that all this was God's will, one reason there was so little resistance. In 1843 between a third and a half of ministers walked out of the Church of Scotland over this issue of patronage, to me one of the greatest moral gestures of our history. The Croik proprietor was serving with his regiment in Australia and, as so often, the factor, Gillanders, was left to do the dirty work.

The baffled and beaten people, (there were 23 children under ten), scratched on the window panes words that still tingle the scalp: 'Glencalvie people was in the church[yard] here May 24, 1845 ...' ...'Glencalvie Greenyard Murder was in the year 1854 March 31' ...'Glencalvie is a wilders ... below sheep that ... to the ... Croick' ... 'Glencalvie people the wicked generation ...' A few were given wretched plots near the east coast, the rest simply vanished, to the cities, to the ships, to their graves. A commissioner was to comment on 'the cold, calculating heartlessness ... as incredible as it is disgusting'. Too late; the glens are empty. The 'Telford' manse is now a holiday home.

OS 20: 456915

OPPOSITE: The sad window with the scratched inscriptions

MUNLOCHY CLOOTIE WELL

This is the most accessible clootie well in Scotland and lies beside the A832 a kilometre west of Munlochy in the Black Isle near Inverness – though the Black Isle is neither black nor an island.

Originally the well was a sacred spot back in pagan times but on the arrival of Christianity, as with much else, was taken over and became St Curitan's Well. Superstition had it that the site would prove efficacious for all manner of ailments and, symbolising this, a piece of cloth from the infirm would be hung on a tree branch; as it rotted away so would the illness involved fade away. Clootie is just a Scots word for piece of cloth. (A tea towel is a dish cloot.) Today's display shows what a superstitious – and ignorant – people we still are with every tree just inside the wood festooned with rags and every manner of garments – many made of nylon which, of course, won't easily rot away.

The site has been changed several times in my lifetime so the well has been pushed back into the wood rather than being on the busy roadside. A car park has been created and a path wends along to the every-growing spectacle. It would be very bad luck to try and remove any offering. I've also found clootie wells at nearby Avoch (Cragie Well) and at Culloden across the Moray Firth (St Mary's) an unusual concentration of a rare feature. Ian Rankin brings Clootie Wells into his Rebus thriller, The Naming of the Dead.

From Inverness cross the Kessock Bridge, A9 northbound, and turn right at the first – Tore – roundabout onto the A832 eastwards. The well lies 4km on, right hand side of the road.

OS 26: 640536

5

MACKENZIE'S SACRIFICE

Roderick Mackenzie was an Edinburgh merchant who joined the forces of Prince Charles Edward Stewart. A fugitive from the slaughter following the Battle of Culloden (1746) he was surprised by redcoats in Glen Moriston. He put up a fight but was eventually overpowered and killed by some very excited soldiers. They had taken him for the Prince! He bore an uncanny resemblance to Prince Charles and he played up to this, with his last words gasping, "You have killed your Prince". His head was struck off for there was a large reward for the Prince, dead or alive, and it was forwarded for identification to Inverness (or London, some sources say). Whatever, it did create what must have been a vital pause in the extensive search for the Prince who eventually made his escape to France.

The spot is marked by a cairn above the A887 road level, about 22.5km west of Invermoriston. Lay-by parking. What many miss is his grave which lies opposite the cairn, below road level, next to the river.

OS 34: 237112

MONSTER MIDGE

Someone obviously had certain feelings about midges. Or nightmares. The granite beastie certainly lies in the midgy west, an area quite unlike anywhere else in Scotland with the vast bogs and ragged sea coast. Ardtoe is a tiny hamlet and not far before reaching it stands this monument to the midge.

The A861 breaks off the Fort William-Mallaig A830 road at Lochailort and makes a great circuit of the districts of Moidart, Sunart and Ardgour (passing the Corran Ferry) to reach the A830 again six kilometres east of Glenfinnan. At the north end of the hamlet Acharacle (which lies at the west end of long Loch Shiel) the B8004, left, is signposted for Kentra and is the road. Kentra is an un-named cluster of houses in the vast moss (bog). A junction for Newton is passed then in the final convulsions after the jetty brae this creatures lies in ambush. Ardtoe has a small strand and parking area. If you head north from Acharacle on the A861 after crossing the Shiel Bridge first left (Dorlin) leads to the larger strand and the spectacular Castle Tioram (Chirum). If wanting to know more about this enemy Alasdair Roberts *Midges* has been reprinted – and tells all. Sadly, the only remedy is emigration.

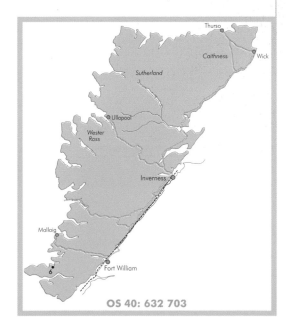

OS 40: 632 703

KIRK ON THE SHORE

Early in the C19 the Church of Scotland was rent over debates about patronage, the system whereby the landowner had the right to appoint a parish minister rather than the congregation doing so. In 1843 nearly half of congregations walked out rather than tolerate this injustice further, an act of considerable courage.

Many intransigent landowners did their utmost to deny the secessionist Free Church (not to be confused with today's fundamentalist 'Wee Frees') any land on which to built a church so expedients were often necessary. At Strontian not even a spot on the shore was allowed and a wooden ark was anchored offshore to act as church. Here we see an auditorium created on the sea's edge to serve the same purpose. The rock seats must have been even harder than church pews and no doubt midges would attend services. At Cove, Loch Ewe (near Gairloch) services following the Disruption were held in a cave, with wooden benches and a pulpit installed. This major rift was only healed in 1929, with a few minority groups of dissent lingering on.

The site, called locally the Church of Ploc is on Am-ploc (the lump) a small jut of land sticking out into the sea at the NE corner of the head of Loch Torridon, a few minutes walk from the road at Fasag.

OS 24: 895561

8

ACHFARY'S TELEPHONE BOX

Telephone boxes were always red, at least before the anaemic current style was introduced which, as well as anything else, was the death blow to the Kirkintilloch foundry that made the red ones. Always red? Well, nearly always; I've read about a black telephone box on the island of Eigg and seen this black and white one which stands on a quiet road in Sutherland with the mighty midget of Ben Stack looming in the background – the hill which received sudden publicity in August 2005 when the former Foreign Secretary, Robin Cook, died while walking on the hill.

Achfary is only an estate hamlet at the end of Loch More and the telephone box stands at the side of the stables by the A838.

I have more recently come on another black telephone box which is sited at Dorlinn on the small road from near Acharacle which runs down to the sea and Castle Tioram. What's more, it is shown on the map. OS40: 644 714.

OS 15: 292396

9

BALNAKEIL

Balnakeil comes from the Gaelic Baile na Cille, *church village*, and a church has stood there for over a thousand years. The ruin is C17 and set in the south wall, with a skull and crossbones symbol, is the grave of Donald MacLeod who was a notorious local clan hit man and highwayman who it is reckoned killed nearly a score of victims. The minister wasn't too happy at having him interred in consecrated ground, hence this site, a compromise perhaps, only half in the church (OS 9: 391686).

 But the incongruous oddity about Balnakeil is the World War Two radar station camp which has been turned into a craft village. (The flat-roofed, whitewashed blocks with blunt towers couldn't have been anything else.) Trees, shrubs and flowers have come on a bit since those days. I almost laughed when I heard a visitor call it 'oddly attractive'. It is also wide ranging and productive: ceramics, silks, woodturning, jewellery, knitwear, soaps, stained glass, handmade books, paintings, prints – the list is endless. The Balnakeil Bistro and the Loch Croisipol bookshop/Restaurant are good eateries, the latter with new and second-hand books. There's also a chocolatier/café. Most open daily, April-October, some all year.

The challenging site lies just west of Durness on the minor road to Balnakeil – beyond which lie magnificent dunes and sands out to Faraid Head. The simple SYHA hostel east of the village is also in wartime huts.

OS 9: 393679

BRAGAR'S WHALEBONE ARCH

A blue whale came ashore at the village of Bragar on the west coast of Lewis in 1922, reputedly the largest whale seen in the Northern hemisphere. It caused quite a stir and, before long, quite a smell, and one Murdo Morrison, the local postmaster, had the lower jaw bones rescued and set up at the back gate of his house. Pillars were built and the huge jaws formed an archway over the gate. From the apex hung the harpoon that had killed the whale.

There was a whaling station at that time on Harris and one of their boats had harpooned this creature only for it to escape and, no doubt, face a lingering death. Harpoons had an explosive charge in their heads but in this case the charge had not gone off. While the local blacksmith was working on the harpoon it did go off, the harpoon embedding itself in the smiddy wall. Lord Leverhulme thought it would look good as the entrance to his castle and offered £1000 for it. No sale. A few years ago the arch was renovated and the centenary of its arrival is not so far ahead. Whalebone arches became quite popular on Scotland's east coast but many have disintegrated over the years. The Jawbone Walk in the Meadows, Edinburgh, still has such an arch at its south end.

Bragar is a long village of working crofts on the A858 West Side coast road. The arch is situated in a garden on the seaward side.

The next village east from Bragar is Arnol where there's Arnol Black House, one of the many saved from the one-time village and authentically restored while, further on southwards, off Carloway (c. 11km) is the restored village of Garenin. Abandoned in 1974 the houses have been usefully reconstructed: there are two self-catering cottage, café and toilets. Just two kilometres on is Dun Carloway broch with its visitor centre and nine kilometres more leads to the standing stones of Callanish (Calanais) so this stretch of coast has the greatest collection of Lewis treasures.

OS 8: 292477

THE UIG TREASURE

Somewhere in the dunes above the vast sands of Uig Bay (Traigh Uige), sometime in the early C19, someone found a collection of items so rare and valuable that the British Museum rates them as the fifth most valuable objects they hold. The somewhere – sometime – someone is not accidental. Where they were found will never be known, who found them is open to argument and just when cannot even be verified. At least we know they are chess and other game pieces.

A large oak carving based on one of the kings of this hoard stands behind the Ardroil dunes in the area where they were probably found. It was the work of Stephen Howard, commissioned in 2006 by Uig Community Council and the Ardroil Grazing Committee. The display board gives one story of the hoard being found by Malcolm Macleod of Pennydonald in a small stone structure in a sand dune.

Eleven of these chess men are in the National Museum of Scotland, eighty two in the British Museum, none in Lewis. There have been endless agitations over this imbalance but Scotland can hardly complain. The Society of Antiquaries of Scotland (precursor of the Museum) was offered the lot when they were finally brought to public notice but would not purchase them. The BM did, less the eleven which a private buyer had obtained, and eventually these were bought by the NMS. The pieces are almost certainly of Viking origin, about C12, and most are made of walrus tusk 'ivory'. There is nothing like them anywhere and they are exquisite. A major exhibition of them toured Scottish cities in 2010.

Having seen them a pilgrimage to where they were found is almost essential. The OS hardly help as Ardroil does not appear on the map though the hamlet is named on road signs and a sign points down the small road to the sands. The big figure is obvious and the road goes on to car parks (and toilets) beside the acres and acres of sand.

When the A858 from Stornoway reaches the West Side (3km before Callanish) turn off onto the B8011 and follow it to its end. The last two kilometres run through a tight pass of disintegrating rocks. Keeping left the continuing small road leads to Ardroil, turning right leads to the Uig Heritage Centre where there is more about the chessmen. The British Museum has published a good small guide to the chessmen and their complex story: *The Lewis Chessmen* by James Robinson.

OS 13: 044322

OUR LADY OF THE ISLES

Hew Lorimer's magnificent statue of the Madonna and child stands on the western slopes of Rueval in South Uist above the A865 main N-S road. The hill is crowned with the large 'golf balls' and masts of a communications centre, and the statue is also clear enough from the road. Pity about all the poles and wires. A short road leads up to the contemplative site.

Hew Lorimer (1907-1993) was the second son of the famous Arts and Crafts architect, Sir Robert Lorimer (Thistle Chapel, Scottish National War Memorial), whose brother John was a successful painter. All three are important in the story of the family-restored Kelly Castle and Garden in East Fife (OS 59: 520052, now NTS). Hew Lorimer studied at Edinburgh College of Art and with Eric Gill. Kelly Castle passed to Hew and he set up his studio in the stable block – where much of his work can be seen, including a miniature version (maquette) of this famous work.

Our Lady of the Isles (9m tall) has his elongated, semi-naturalistic style. It was carved on site from the almost white Creetown granite and is an eye-catcher from afar. It is worth going further up the hill to look down on the sweeping panorama over which the figures gaze. The statue is also a useful seamark.

Father John Morrison, a local priest, commissioned the Rueval sculpture which was paid for by local people and consecrated in 1958. Part of the inspiration too was to try and thwart the MOD who wanted to take over the whole north side of the island for their rocket range – itself now history. There is a somewhat similar mother and child group half way up Heaval (Sheabhal) above Castlebay on Barra known as Our Lady, Star of the Sea. The babe holds a star aloft. It is the work of Maxwell Allan. (OS 31: 679992)

OS 22: 776407

BOAT IN CHURCH

St Michael's of the Sea Church in Eriskay has a 'clean-gleaming' interior besides a great setting up on a hill overlooking the Kyle of Eriskay and the causeway to South Uist. The unusual here is the altar which incorporates the bows of a boat (a lifeboat which had been washed overboard from HMS *Hermes*). Outside hangs a ship's bell from the German battle-cruiser *Derfflinger* which was scuttled in Scapa Flow in 1919 and salvaged in 1939, but then was anchored upside down during the war before being broken up on the Clyde in 1946, the last of the scuttled fleet to be salvaged.

The church was built by Father Allan, a notable collector of old lore at the end of the C19. (The island was famed for its musical traditions and the beautiful *Eriskay Love Lilt* is world-famous.) The church was built by the islanders under Father Allan's guidance with wood from wrecks, shore sand, cement full of shells and the plentiful local stone.

I was shocked later to read that the *Derfflinger* bell had been handed back to the German navy on their visit to the Clyde in the 1960s and is now in a German Naval Academy museum in Flensburg. Father Roddy McAuley, the parish priest for St Michael's was able to clarify this seeming anomaly. There were two bells.

Eriskay also has a place in history as it was here that the ill-favoured Charles Edward Stewart (Bonnie Prince Charlie) first set foot on Scottish soil. When it was suggested he went home he is supposed to have retorted "I have come home". But Eriskay I'm sure is best known thanks to the 1948 film *Whisky Galore*, based on Compton Mackenzie's book which was based on a true incident during World War Two. The 12,000 ton steamship *The Politician* was sneaking through the Outer Hebrides on the way to New York when she went aground off Eriskay (1941). Among her cargo were 264,000 bottles of whisky. The locals took this as treasure trove but then two agents of HM Customs & Excise arrived on the scene. Much was hidden (and some still occasionally surfaces from a rabbit burrow or other hidey-hole). What the film didn't show was how 36 islanders (including a boy of 14) were sent to court by the excisemen and nineteen served sentences in Inverness prison. Oddly, Eriskay only had its first pub open in 1988. It is named *Am Politician*. I love the way one thing leads to another.

If on Eriskay do climb its summit, Beinn Scrien (Sciathan), only 185 metres, but a magical viewpoint with Barra to the south, the rest of the isles as hill on hill to the north, Rum crouched to the east, and, as I had it, a golden sunset over the sea westwards.

OS 31: 786120

RUM ISLAND

'A pink elephant'; that was how W H Murray described Kinloch Castle on the island of Rum. The castle has indeed proved a bit of a white elephant and is desperately needing restoration – any millionaire readers please help. Rum was bought in 1887 by John Bullough, a wealthy Victorian industrialist from the Midlands who was succeeded by his son George, the archetypal Edwardian, who built the castle, owned a world-cruising yacht and created ostentatious oddities like a turtle pool and orangery at the castle. The name was changed to Rhum as Rum didn't quite sound the thing. To grow anything, soil was brought in from Ayrshire and the castle is built of Arran sandstone. The Lancashire workers were all issued with kilts while on Rum – no doubt to the appreciation of the midges.

The inside of the castle was built with every mod. con: a private hydro scheme for electricity, a mechanical orchestra under the grand stairway to entertain diners, a library with books bought by the yard, baths which were forerunners of the jacuzzi ... and all this on a Hebridean island from which they did their best to ban visitors. It took a hundred employees to keep one family comfortable on their periodic visits. The laundry was situated seven kilometres away at Kilmory. The glory departed with the First World War. By 1936 the island's population was twenty. The castle, however, isn't the oddest feature.

John Bullough had been buried at Harris in a vault with tile decorations that someone compared to a railway toilet. Piqued, Sir George had a proper mausoleum built, a startlingly incongruous little Greek temple, where his father, himself and his wife could lie in state for ever.

Sir George (Seoras) died in 1939 and the widowed Lady Bullough sold the island to the then Nature Conservancy Council in 1957. When she died in 1967, aged 98, her coffin was taken to Rum to be interred in the family mausoleum. I happened to be in Harris with a school party when the cortege arrived, something not to be forgotten. One or two of the boys found it even weirder for the night before the gang had been chased off to find somewhere to sleep out as they could and this imaginative pair spread their sleeping bags on the conveniently flat tops of the canopied sarcophagi.

Rum is still an important research station (red deer, woodland restoration, sea eagles re-introduction, etc) and National Nature Reserve, but visitors are welcome. There's a new big pier and various accommodation options: B&B (including the castle), a bothy at Dibidil or camping. (Rum is on OS 39, the castle at Kinloch 401995, Harris: 338959.) Sailings from Mallaig are operated by Caledonia Macbrayne and interconnect the 'Small Isles': Rum, Eigg, Muck and Canna (tel. Mallaig, 01687-462 403) and there are also sailings from Arisaig (Arisaig Marine, tel. 01687-450 224).

OS Sheet 39

A TIDAL LOO

Isle Oronsay or Ornsay or, more correctly, Eilean Iarmain, lies on the Skye shore of the Sound of Sleat (pronounced *Slate*) off the A851 road down the Sleat Peninsula to the Armadale-Mallaig ferry. The name appears about a score of times in the west for it is the Viking name for a tidal island. The island here shelters a bay and what at one time was a busy hamlet – still one of the finest and unspoilt in Skye. The line of crofts runs south to Camus Croise with its beach. There's a hotel, art gallery and various other dockside buildings which have been converted or restored and the pier (drystane) has a rare surviving hand crane.

A one-time 'gazebo' was in fact a sea-flushing lavatory and though converted to a doocot in the 1990's its original fittings and functions are retained. It is the small white square building with a pyramid slated roof, well seen and accessible from the pier. A visit at high tide is the most interesting. Balfour harbour on Shapinsay, Orkney also has a tidal loo which I've not seen mentioned anywhere (see p7).

The lighthouse buildings on Eilean Sionnach, off Ornsay, were at one time owned by Gavin Maxwell and the view looks across towards Sandaig, his 'Camusfearna', backed by Beinn Sgritheal and the Rough Bounds of Knoydart. (The isle itself, Isle Ornsay, is on Sheet 33.)

It was in the bay here that Flora Macdonald who had helped Bonnie Prince Charlie escape from the Hebrides was captured by the frigate *Unicorn* and duly ended in the Tower of London.

OS 32: 702123

ONE MAN'S ROAD

Raasay suffered as badly as anywhere during the C19 Clearances with whole hamlets being left devoid of people. Many were forced to the north end of Raasay and the desolation of Rona beyond, land too poor for the greedy landowners to grab. After WW2 – under kindlier circumstances – the drift south picked up and slowly the north end drained of its people. One contributing factor was the lack of a road over the last few miles from Brochel Castle (illustrated), that rotten fang of stone that stands against the gape of sea. Beyond were only rough tracks. When electricity came to Raasay the supplies stopped short too. When the school closed the children had to walk and there's one story where, returning from school, they were dropped miles short because of snow and simply left to fend as they could. They sheltered behind a rock till rescued.

As long ago as the 1920's petitions had been made for a road but the various councils, dominated by landowners, procrastinated and opposed in what would be Clearances by default. There were not many votes in Arnish. In 1964 Calum MacLeod, in his sixties, loaded a wheelbarrow with tools and set off to build the road himself, on top of his normal work as light keeper and crofter. There were still seven families when he started, a decade later when he would drive a Land Rover over his road, there was just him and his wife. What he called 'infamous maladministrations' over half a century had won. A whole Gaelic culture and way of life was disappearing. At this stage the authorities began to think something should be done for north Raasay!

Much of the pressure came from Calum's heroic task which was recognized everywhere as sadly symbolic as well as defiant. 'Calum's Road' became known worldwide in the diaspora of the islanders. But it took the authorities another decade to get the tarmac down and twenty passing places made. (An estimate could take so long in the procedural maze that it was then invalidated by inflated costs.) But it is there now and life improved at once. Calum enjoyed six years of the road, dying in 1988. He was a scholar, writer and innovator, fluent in Gaelic and English – the languages on the tribute cairn at the top of the road I saw above Brochel Castle.

I very happily took my camper van down Calum's Road which is steep and tortuous, as the landscape dictates, but perfectly engineered. I enjoyed a day afoot in a world marvellously remote and peaceful then drove out again, lifting a metaphorical hat to a wonderful man. Do get a hold of Roger Hutchinson's book *Calum's Road* (Birlinn 2006) and read about the whole astonishing saga. You will rage and you will cheer.

Raasay is reached by vehicle ferry from Sconser in Skye and the start of Calum's Road lies 14km to the north, a memorable drive too.

OS Sheet 24

ARDCLASH BELL TOWER

This is the finest detached bell tower (belfry) in Scotland, a C17 gem in an out-of-this-world, tranquil setting high above the River Findhorn, in a crook of which nestles a small church. The tower was built first as prison and watch tower but so scattered was the parish that a bell rung at the church was never heard – so it was added to the tower. In those unsettled days a warning bell could be a lifesaver.

The last miles of the road approach give a delightful run through the wooded Findhorn world. Coming from the south the B9007 (an old military road) is taken from Carrbridge, over moorland above Lochindorb with its castle the one time lair of the Wolf of Badenoch, then turns off left for dramatic Dulsie Bridge (Wade, 1750), right at a fork soon after and then right again after 1.5km. After 3km once more turn right and quickly right again at the big new church for the last 600m to the track to the bell tower. From the north take the A939 from Nairn for about 10km and turn off, right, at Redburn where the bell tower is signposted (Historic Scotland). After 1.5km it is a left and right to the bell tower track. There is no real parking and neither the track nor road should be blocked. Turning is not easy. For the fit the easy option is to take the hairpin bends down to the old church where there is plenty of parking space.

The church is closed but the graveyard still in use. A stone outside the wall suggests a suicide's grave and a flat slab has a visible date 1670. Several stones with some artistic effort are for members of the Findhorn community. There are also two identical stones from a man who married twice and obviously was being impartial. On the track for the bell tower is a monument to the Rev. Donald Mitchell, b.1792, son of the local minister, who became, perhaps, Scotland's first missionary to India. The Mission to Lepers erected the monument in 1961 and the site in India is still a Church of Scotland leprosarium.

Shortly after the monument, on the left, there is a gate and a steep path/steps leading up to the bell tower. The initial surprise is how small the tower is, only 4.3m square. And watch your head on the doorway. A straight stair leads up to a room with a fireplace, small windows and shot holes, from where watch could be kept. The room below with no windows could have held prisoners. The belfry is on the south gable and there is a date 1655. A monogram MGB over the fireplace is for the Brodies of Lethen, Alexander, the builder, as a Covenanter, was much harried and his estate plundered (once by the Marquis of Montrose) – so had need of a watch tower.

OS 27: 953453

2

PORTRAIT OF A FAKER

One of the oddest exhibits in the Clan Macpherson Museum in Newtonmore is a portrait of James Macpherson (1736-1796) – which is painted on glass! But odder still is the person portrayed for this was the man responsible for the longest-running literary spat in British history. Dr Johnson was one of the scoffers about Macpherson's work and so rancorous were the communications between the two men that the doctor started carrying a cudgel when out of doors. On the other hand Goethe compared Macpherson with Shakespeare, Sheridan ranked him with Homer, Thomas Jefferson rated him the greatest poet ever and Napoleon never travelled without 'Ossian' in his baggage. The Romantic poets, novelists, playwrights, painters, musicians, soldiers and statesmen all bowed at this altar. Scotland, longing for a past glory to counter the recent dismal years, went overboard. Stories of untainted, primitive civilizations, 'the Noble Savage', were Rousseau realised. Macpherson's timing was brilliant. He hurried out a sequel!

Macpherson had a very chequered career, Boswellian ups and downs, MP for the rotten burgh of Cameltord in Devon at one time, but he still retired to Strathspey to build the mansion of Balavil, today glimpsed from the A9 heading north about 2.5km from Kingussie. The sad thing is that he had actually done some quite notable collecting but then creatively doctored his material to gain greater kudos. David Hume's eventual judgment of the works was of 'a palpable and impudent forgery'. Macpherson had travelled in Mull, Skye and the Outer Hebrides (with a Gaelic-speaking poet cousin) and he did collect folklore and hear ballads recited, material, which presented genuinely would have been received kindly. Instead he worked on the material with marvellous invention to produce a book-length poem, supposedly translated from manuscripts, by C3 Fingal's son Ossian. *Fingal, an Epic* appeared in 1761 and *Temora* followed. It was all a bit blatant: the story had a Scots Fingal invading Ulster c.200AD to aid the fight against invading Norsemen – a reversal of the real population (and folklore) movement and six centuries before the earliest Norse incursion. But it was the continuing failure to produce the manuscripts that had heavyweights like Hume, Johnson, Scott step aside from the general enthusiasm. (There are no manuscripts before C9/C10.) So, the potential collector and scholar became the acknowledged faker. Irony too, both he and Johnson now lie under the same roof – in Westminster Abbey.

Newtonmore is now bypassed by the A9 but clearly signposted and the Museum is situated at the southern end of the main street, where the A86 Great Glen road breaks off. Open: Easter to October. Tel: 01540-712323.

OS35: 788023

3

CRANNOG, LOCH TAY

Looking at maps the word *crannog* appears on Scottish lochs from Shetland to Galloway (and in Ireland) and are thought to date back to 5000 years ago. Some were lived in as recently as the C17. They were simply safe or, at least, safer dwellings through obviously turbulent times, being surrounded by water and connected by causeway or stepping stones to the shore. The remarkable thing about them is their being built on platforms supported by poles up to ten metres long driven in to the bed of the loch. How did they do that?

The icy, peaty waters of Scottish lochs have preserved quite a lot of material from crannogs (an odd branch of underwater archaeology if you like), things like seeds of cherry, bramble, raspberry, domestic goats, sheep and cattle remains, besides pottery, stone tools, a leather bucket and a butter dish with butter still sticking to the inside. Today many appear as woody islets or small heaps of stone (original infill). There are more than a dozen round Loch Tay.

The Oakbank Crannog near Fearnan on Loch Tay has been extensively researched and has led to the reconstruction of a crannog. This became an instant tourist attraction. Most visitors are astonished at the building's size, efficiency, dryness, strength and construction details. I certainly was. There's an on-shore exhibition and hands-on experiences besides the marvel of the crannog itself.

The Scottish Crannog Centre lies on the south shore of Loch Tay not far from Kenmore (reached by the A827 off the A9). Open mid March – end November, 10.00-17.30 (16.00 in November). Tel: 01887-830583.

OS 52: 770449

DUNKELD'S ELL

At the far end of the attractive old square at Dunkeld the eye is caught by 'The Ell Shop' but few realise why it is so called. On the corner where the road goes on to the cathedral an iron rod, forked at both ends, is the actual ell, a rare survivor of its type.

Today, despite our half step towards metrics, we talk about 'give a man an inch and he'll take a mile'. In 1706 when this ell was forged you might have heard, 'Aye, gie'm an inch an he'll take an ell'. The ell was a measure, in Scotland standardised in 1661 as 37 inches. Market places would have official ones by which merchants could test their own. Parliament passed an act in 1824 to standardise measurements so the ell fell out of use and few have survived. This one is dated 1706 and bears the initials AD.

Dunkeld lies off the busy A9 about fifteen miles north of Perth, reached over a bridge built by Thomas Telford. There's a large car park through the village, which becomes busy in the tourist season as it (with Birnam across the Tay) enjoys a beautiful setting in the heart of Perth's Big Tree Country. There is also an ell in the graveyard at Dornoch Cathedral (OS21: 799895).

OS 52: 24426

5
WATER TOWER AS ART GALLERY

Years ago I photographed this building simply because it was oddly distinctive but had no idea of its history. A round, parapet-rimmed stone building, but, above that, a domed rotunda with blind windows and topped off with a tall column with an urn on top – which proved to be a chimney. Very odd. The rotunda and dome is actually the cast iron tank of Perth's first – 1832 – waterworks. It held 146,000 gallons (over 66,000 litres). It remained as a pumping station till 1965 and is Scotland's earliest known cast iron building and possibly the oldest such surviving anywhere. The motto over the door, *Aquam Igne et aqua haurio* translates *By Fire and Water Draw Water*. The site was once that of the castle built by Cromwell when he rampaged his forces through Scotland. Many precious early gravestones from the nearby Greyfriars graveyard were pillaged for his fort. In 1992 the waterworks building was turned into the attractive Fergusson Gallery, showing the extensive collection of works by the versatile Scottish colourist J D Fergusson (1874-1961). A 1918 bronze *Torse de Femme* by the artist stands in front of the entrance.

The Fergusson Gallery stands at the corner of Tay Street and Marshall Place facing the South Inch, the vast parkland on that side of the city. There is extensive parking on the Inch or the road by the river. Tel: 01738-441944.

OS 58: 119231

6
SADDLING THE GREY MARE

That is how a friend from the area described this oddity in the Sma' Glen by the River Almond. Books and internet create a confusion over the name and purpose so I'll stick to local opinion. In 1867 the site was suddenly called Clach Ossian, really a site two kilometres further on, the OS map has it as Giant's Grave, some have it Soldier's Grave, but it is not a grave. The legend then.

Beside this large boulder (one of several in the trees after all) is a smaller stone – the size that most of us would wisely not attempt to lift. But 'to saddle the grey mare' that is just what has to be done: the small stone lifted and placed on top of the large one. That is all, no doubt a bit of fun going back many years.

I've personal experience of how distortions can arise. As a boy our gang, for our own convenience, named a boulder above Castle Campbell in the Ochils as 'William's Stone'. Decades on I saw a book on the area in which it was speculated the name had something to do with William the Lion! I have not saddled the Grey Mare.

The stone lies just down the bank among the trees from the A822 road 1.5km from the junction with the B8063.

OS 52: 904295

7
EARTHQUAKE HOUSE

The small town of Comrie lies on the Highland boundary fault at a spot once unusually prone to earthquakes. In the 1830s local seismologists recorded 7300 tremors, 'sometimes accompanied by a loud report and sulphurous smells'. Notable quakes were in 1839 (a score of shocks in 24 hours) and 1875 and the most recent of note in 1965. Fissures could appear but remarkably little damage to property occurred. A road in Perth, 32km to the east once cracked and caused subsidence. The small square stone Earthquake House was set up in 1874 by the (deep breath) British Association's Committee for the Investigation of Scottish and Irish Earthquakes but, with the then falling off in the number of quakes, was eventually abandoned. In 1988 the building was restored and equipped with modern instruments by the British Geological Survey. One peers in through a glass panel doorway as footsteps on entry could actually cause a recordable tremor! A model of the original Mallet seismometer can be seen. The first historical reference to earthquakes here was in 1597.

Heading west out of 'the Skakey toun' on the A85 Lochearnhead road, turn off left over the picturesque 1792 Bridge of Ross. Take the left fork (Dalrannoch) and the Earthquake House will be seen above a field on the right. Park and take a path just beyond the first house up to an access gate.

OS 52: 765217

MACKONOCHIE'S CROSS

This lies by the vast Blackwater Reservoir up in the hills east of Kinlochleven – from where it is reached by a pleasant walk. The dam is a sad spot with the graves of unknown navies below its wall. From the north end of the dam a rough path heads off through the hills to Loch Treig. After 1km it leaves the reservoir and heads up the Allt an Inbhir where the map-marked 'monument' is seen across the burn.

'Who was the Alexander Heriot Mackonochie?' I'd long wanted to know and, oddly, found the answer in a book I bought in Shetland. There was the story – in execrable doggerel – which could have been the work of William McGonagall. When I reached the last of the 17 stanzas I laughed. It *was* by McGonagall. So

Friends of humanity, of high and low degree,/I pray ye all come listen to me;/And truly I will relate to ye,/The tragic fate of the Rev Alexander Heriot Mackonochie.

Who was on a visit to the Bishop of Argyle,/ For the good of his health, for a short while;/ Because for the last three years his memory had been affected, / Which prevented him from getting his thoughts collected.

In December, 1887, this man, who seems to have had a mental breakdown, set out on a known walk accompanied by a Skye terrier, a deer-hound and the Bishop's two dogs. The bishop was not concerned until dinner time came with no sign of the reverend. Two men were sent to search. Nothing.

And when the bishop heard it, he procured a carriage and pair, / While his heart was full of woe, and in a state of despair:/ He organized three search parties without delay, / And headed one of the parties in person without dismay.

Two parties set off with lamps *Mr Mackonochie to try and find, / In the midst of driving hail, and the howling wind.* Mamore Lodge and the Devil's Staircase were searched, a party also ascending from the Glencoe side. In equally bad weather search was resumed next morning, the worthy bishop *Accompanied with a crowd of men and dogs, / All resolved to search the forest and the bogs.* The dogs proved their worth. *Then the party pressed on right manfully, / And sure enough there were the dogs guarding the body of Mackonochie; / And the corpse was cold and stiff, having been long dead. / Alas! almost frozen, and a wreath of snow around the head. And as the searchers gathered round the body in pity they did stare, /Because his right foot was stained with blood, and bare; / But when the Bishop o'er the corpse had offered up a prayer, / He ordered his party to carry the corpse to his house on a bier.*

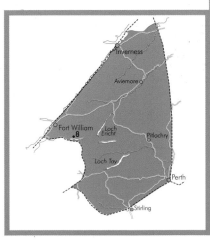

9

SECRET PORTRAIT

In the West Highland Museum, situated in Cameron Square in the centre of Fort William, is an odd exhibit which dates to the C18 period of Jacobite rebellions or their aftermath when any connection or sign of support for the exiled Stewarts was treasonable. All sorts of subterfuges were thought up. A toast would be made "To the king!" but the glasses would be raised over a bowl of water, in other words, 'the king over the water', their James in France or Italy and not Hanoverian George in London.

The strangest of these subterfuges is found in the museum. What would simply look like some swirls of paint on a disc and a shiny cylinder would mean nothing if either was found; bring them together though, stand the cylinder on the disc and there appears a portrait of Bonnie Prince Charlie. There is no record of who made or owned this curiosity which was discovered by the founder of the Museum quite by chance (both bits apart) in a London junk shop. It is now one of the gems of the extensive Jacobite collection on display.

The museum is open all year: Mon-Sat 10-4 or 5, and Sun 2-5 in July, August. Tel. 01397-702169

Opposite: The Secret Portrait revealed
Below: The meaningless paint marks on the disc

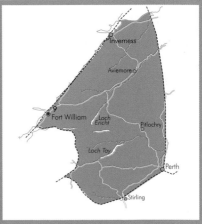

LOST IN THE LOSSIE FOREST

Here we have the weird sight of a coastal anti-tank barrier of concrete blocks seemingly running through the heart of an inland forest. But when they were erected they were coastal; the forest did not exist, which pushes World War Two ever further back into memories. You can see the same thing at Tentsmuir Forest in Fife. Being taken over by forestry plantings in such a fashion has helped to preserve the barriers. After the war, on better agricultural land, farmers were encouraged to remove defence sites by being paid a bounty. (£5 for a pillbox.) Cramond Island in the Forth Estuary had a 0.5km line of blocks connecting it to the shore in order to prevent enemy submarines sneaking through the gap, which still exists.

The easiest route to see an impressive section of these old defences (and popular with local dog-walkers) is from near the map-named Arthur's Bridge on the B9103 from Lossiemouth to the A96 between Elgin and Lhanbryde. Arthur's Bridge actually spans the River Lossie but about 250m SE of it a forestry road off east crosses a bridge over the Innes Canal (OS28: 255670). There are no signs but take this and just within the forest (past houses) is a car park on the left. The track from the back of the parking area puts in a couple of bends then runs straight for 1.5km to lead right to the line of blocks where there is a machine gun post as well (OS 28: 267683). To the right the blocks twist up and down through the pre-war dunes to another blockhouse and then, seemingly, on for ever. Signposts indicate routes to Lossiemouth. Out ands back takes about an hour but other circuits could be made.

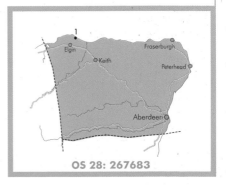

OS 28: 267683

GIANT'S STEPS

These are on Logie Head, 2km NE of Cullen on the Moray coast, a popular spot for rock climbing on the seashore dykes. A Cullen man, Tony Hetherington, spent the summer of 1987 rebuilding a ruinous flight of steps, shifting huge blocks of quartzite, some of which had fallen to the foot of the climb, without any lifting tackle or mechanical aids, a feat which compares with the work to restore the Whalligoe Steps (p.13). Hetherington died in a canoeing accident in 1993; there is a memorial cairn and plaque to him at the foot of the steps. Cullen is an attractive town built as a planned village by the Earl of Seafield early in the C19.

From Cullen you can start either high at the Caravan Park or low at the harbour, the former edges the cliff and has a viewpoint (Nelson's Seat) before the path descends to the bay, the latter passes a distinctly odd cemetery – for pets. After rimming the bay the path twists up and down and up over the seaward-running dykes, then drops again in the impressive Giant's Steps. Not a route to take in a high wind! Return the same way or on a bit and cut up by a path to the ruin of Logie House and so back to Cullen. If transport can be arranged it is worth continuing round Sunnyside Bay to the startling view onto the Lindlater Castle ruins then inland by a 'beehive' doocot to parking at the abandoned farm, Barnyards – or keep to the coastal path on to delectable Sandend Bay and village. Splendid scenery throughout. You may see Morven in Caithness, over fifty miles away.

OS 29: 529681

OSTRICH FOUNTAIN

Fraserburgh (The Broch to locals) has one of the most highly decorated cast-iron fountains in the country. The intricate pattern of the dome is as fine as filigree but the really odd – unique – feature is the crowning figure of an ostrich with a key in its beak. I made the mistake of asking why. Apparently it came from the town crest (the key to the town symbolism) but this still didn't answer why an ostrich. Originally a horseshoe in an ostrich's beak was intended for the town crest but this was too close to Lord Saltoun's coat of arms so they changed it to the key. This just shifted the question back: why did Lord Saltoun's coat of arms have an ostrich? As Lord Saltoun did not know I rather gave up at that point. And don't ask me why the town is The Broch. Everyone told me – giving different reasons.

The fountain dates to 1904 and originally would have had an eagle on top but that was stopped and the ostrich with key was cast instead. The commission came from the Town Council and Feuars managers. The town's coat of arms was never registered so was strictly speaking illegal – till they petitioned the Lord Lyon King of Arms in 1930 for an authorised version.

Entering Fraserburgh by the A90 there's an industrial area, long hedges (masking playing fields) on both sides, war memorial, left, then the very obvious Fountain in a garden, right (Saltoun Place Gardens.) The fountain originally occupied the spot where the war memorial stands and was moved in 1923. There's a big, fascinating Heritage Centre (tel: 01346-512888) facing the Lighthouse Museum (tel: 01346-511022), both worth taking time to visit.

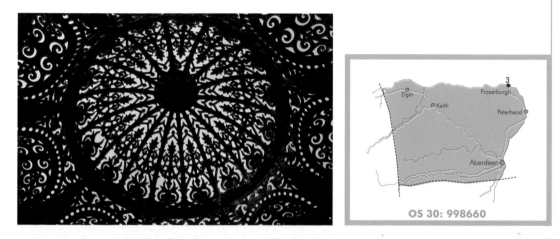

OS 30: 998660

CRIMOND

Crimond is a village on the A90 Fraserburgh to Peterhead road but the name is known worldwide as the most popular tune to which the Twenty Third Psalm is sung. (The Lord's My Shepherd …). It was composed by Jessie Seymour, daughter of the local minister in 1872.

Crimond's real oddity however is the clock on the kirk, inscribed 'The Hour's Coming'; this shows an hour of sixty one minutes. The clockmaker inadvertently divided the last five minutes to the hour into six parts. The error was corrected in a repainting in 1949 but there was such an outcry that the sixty one minutes were restored. The clock originally was part of a local big house but was given to the church. There is no problem parking; the church is on the east side of the road through the village.

The Lord's my shepherd, I'll not want.
He makes me down to lie
In pastures green: he leadeth me
the quiet waters by.
My soul he doth restore again;
and me to walk doth make
Within the paths of righteousness,
ev'n for his own name's sake.

Yea, though I walk in death's dark vale,
yet will I fear none ill:
For thou art with me; and thy rod
and staff me comfort still.

Stanza 1 and 2 of the 1650 metrical Psalms

OS 30: 054578

AN ART DECO FEATURE IN ABERDEEN

Just off the west end of Aberdeen's Union Street, at the junction of Holburn Street (Union Street's continuation) and Justice Mill Lane stands a pillar of Art Deco appearance. It looks as if it should perhaps have had a clock or bells at the top instead of what you see – so what was it? A memorial was the guess of some passers-by I questioned. Out of mischief I asked ten people and not one knew!

Books were confusing too but early in the C20 (1901-3) the corporation built a subway in connection with the Millburn Street power station and this carried gas supplies. What we see is a humble gas main ventilator, except there is nothing humble about it – a fine example of what was done with cast iron in those days.

Aberdeen's first gas works were in 1824, an early initiative for the go-ahead city. Parking in central Aberdeen being difficult this curiosity is best discovered on foot.

OS 38: 933057

BELL TOWER/WATCH HOUSE

Banchory or Banchory-Ternan to distinguish it from Banchory Devenick just outside Aberdeen, is the largest of the lower Deeside towns and was situated in an intrusive part of Kincardineshire, rather than Aberdeenshire. This oddity was because a Burnett of Leys (of Crathes Castle, now NTS) insisted both Crathes and his other home, Muchalls Castle near Stonehaven shared the same shire! St Ternan, an early Celtic missionary is thought to have founded a colony here in the mid C5.

The old church, now gone, was St Ternan's, and stood down by the river, this oldest part of Banchory now at the town's eastern end. In the kirkyard stands the 1829 white tower 'like a tea caddy' with balancing belfry and chimney on the conical roof. The chimney points to it being a watch house, to keep guard over the graves of the newly buried which ran the risk of being stolen by grave robbers (resurrectionists). The watchers liked to keep warm. The bell came from the former church and was cast in the Netherlands and is dated 1664. The old church was rebuilt in 1775 but in 1824 moved across the road above to the present East Church.

The graveyard lies at the east end of Banchory but is difficult to spot and has dangerous access so driving out of Banchory when you come to traffic lights turn up Raemoir Road and park, then walk. East, soon after the lights, a small, rough lane leads down to the graveyard. Take care crossing the main road. Coming from the Aberdeen direction there is a church with clock tower on the right and an obvious fountain on the left where a lane angles off down to the graveyard, a possibility for small cars, else go on to the lights and turn right up Raemoir Road, park and walk as above.

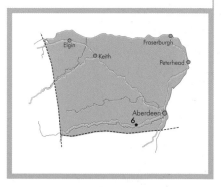

THE BIG SHOT'S CRACK SHOT

In Victorian times the Glen Tanar estate near Aboyne was owned by wealthy William Cunliffe Brooks (1819-1900). His CV reads Rugby and Cambridge, the Middle Temple, Banking and MP. He had homes on Grosvenor Square, Barlow Hall (near Manchester), and Glen Tana. He could afford to follow his enthusiasms.

Among his foibles was a delight in marking any spot of interest on his lands and the oddest of these indicates the place where he shot the Haunted Stag, a name he gave to a beast which long eluded him. He was a fanatic stag-hunter. (The ballroom ceiling at Glen Tanar is still decorated with over 500 sets of antlers.) He finally did shoot this stag, on the moors Hill of Baudy Meg and Duchery Beg, the land between the Firmounth and Fungle tracks, historic routes from Deeside over to Glen Esk.

CB then erected this strange monument to his success: a dumpy stone pyramid topped by a large ball while 81 metres (267 feet) further on another identical marker can be seen on the skyline; the first marks where CB fired the shot, the second where the unlucky stag received the fatal bullet.

Glen Tanar lies SW from Aboyne, from which the Dee is crossed to join the south road westwards for a couple of kilometres to Bridge o' Eas where the multi-coloured entrance and odd gatehouse can hardly be missed. Drive up to a woody parking area with a bridge leading to the Braeloine visitor centre. There are map boards indicating walks and initially our route follows markers to the Knochan viewpoint (indicator). This passes the Chapel of St Lesmo and heads off up the Firmounth track. From the viewpoint continue along the rising track with trees only on the left and, where trees also reappear on the right, take the smaller track angling up through the trees, plantings of larch and Scots pines. Eventually exit the trees and turn left on meeting another track. Follow this as it circles round Baudy Meg, keeping right at a fork. The markers will soon be spotted, lying off left just before the saddle between Meg and the 466 rise. Carnferg's summit monument is prominent. Almost illegible wording on the stones declares 'The haunted stag / The stag is dead. / Sure bullet to its fatal mark hath sped.'

Continue along the track which descends steeply (gritty granite) into old woodland with superb Scots pines and an underspread of juniper. In season, some bird cherries may be festooned with the nests of the destructive Ermine moth caterpillars. The track runs gently along to reach the Knochan viewpoint and 'home' – one of the most demanding walks in this book, best left to regular hillwalkers.

OS 44: 499933

STONEHAVEN FIREBALL FESTIVAL

Thousands line the High Street and harbour area in Stonehaven (Stanehive) to see in the New Year watching this remarkable ceremony. Just under fifty locals take part and parade up and down the High Street swinging flaming balls of fire round their heads before finally lobbing them into the waters of the harbour. The combustible material is in a wire cage with a long handle attached – and each person has their own secret 'recipe'. The origin of this particular festival is not known but it has been a regular event for a century, and apart from the World Wars, has never not taken place.

Perhaps, like the Burryman (p.131), there is an element of purging the old and starting anew in the ceremony. It has been reported elsewhere in the past and quite a few towns still have some form of midwinter bonfire ceremonies. A procession with 'Burning the Clavie' at Burghead is the nearest to Stonehaven's extraordinary spectacle. And spectacle it is.

For the last hour of the Auld Year crowds gather from near and far and wait good humouredly while a pipe band parades a couple of times. One by one the fireballs are lit and at 00.00 they head into the town. And less than half an hour later the remains of the fireballs (flaming, smouldering or even empty cages) arc into the sea. And almost at once, up on the brae beyond the harbour, the fireworks are lit, and I don't think I've ever seen such an attractive display, a great ending for a unique experience.

There's an evening programme in the town square and every hotel and restaurant is kept busy as people flock in. Parking is interesting. You may have a bit of a hike! Then from about ten o'clock there's a steady flow towards the old town.

If making a day of the visit have a walk in the Dunottar Woods where there are several odd features. The one-time mansion has gone but on top of Gallow's Hill there is its ice house, a rare pepperpot shell house folly below the walled garden and Lady Kennedy's Bath upstream: oval walls encircling the burn where her ladyship would splash. West of the wood is the old Dunottar church with a Covenanter's stone on which Scott found a mason at work whom he turned into his Old Mortality.

Stonehaven, the 'county town' of Kincardineshire lies on the coast 24km south of Aberdeen and 37 km north of Montrose and is clearly indicated from the A90.

OS Sheet 45

YOUNGEST, OLDEST, TALLEST, SHORTEST

Women who are married in the parish church at St Cyrus and qualify as youngest, oldest, tallest, shortest in any year are recipients from a dowry set up in 1844 by John Orr of Bridgeton who had worked most of his life in India. His bequest of £1000 was divided into fifths, the first part going to 'purchase sugar, meal, candles, flannel and other comforts' for the needy old folk, the rest available for the four odd, but randomly fair, categories of bride mentioned. As the sums have shrunk in real terms over the decades the brides now receive a trophy instead. Shoes have to come off and piled up hair loosened when the measuring arm is lowered on a head. The stand sits in the church still but, rather sadly, there has been a general drop in church weddings.

There's an illustrated booklet on sale at the church giving the idiosyncratic history of this unique custom. Sunday services are at 10.00.

St Cyrus lies on the A92 Aberdeen road about 8km north of Montrose. The tall steeple is a useful seamark on its cliff top setting. The lane alongside the church leads to the cliffs, with great views, and a challenging path to the sands below. The coastline is a Nature Reserve and there is a small visitor centre.

OS 45: 750648

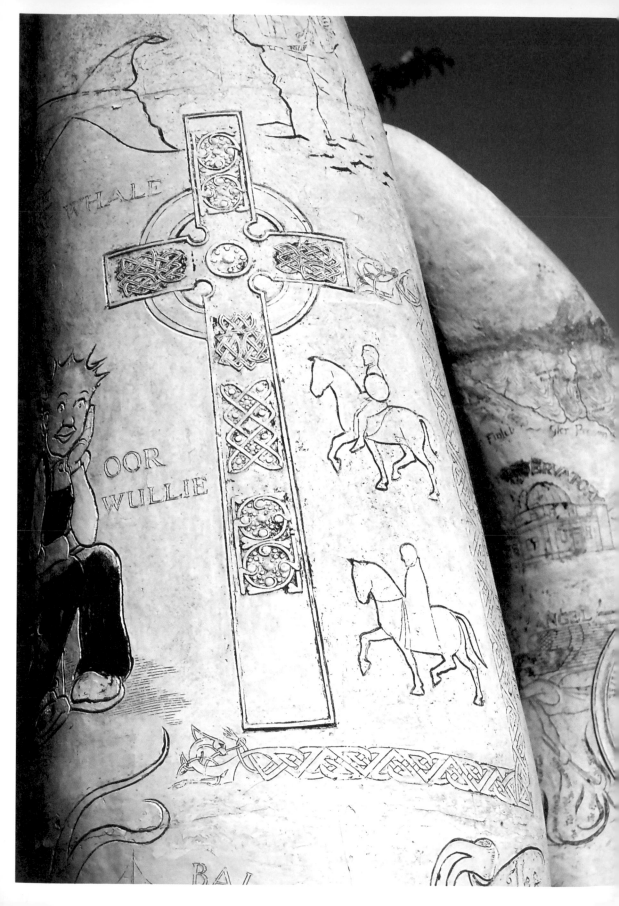

3

TUSKS IN DUNDEE

These are *scrimshaw* writ large and in concrete rather than walrus tusk or ivory. Scrimshaw was the name given to artefacts with drawings, carvings (on tusks, shells etc) made by sailors to pass weary hours at sea in the days of sail. The sailors often had a strong connection with whaling and exploration in high latitudes which is the connection with Dundee, a whaling port, making this odd-looking trio imaginatively apposite. The Dundee Tusks have etched into their surfaces just about everything to do with the city's history, lore and personalities – from a Pictish beast to Mary Slessor to Oor Wullie (and today's graffiti).

They lie just below the busy Lochee Road (buses every few minutes) as it starts to twist up and round the slopes of the Law. Just after passing Dudhope Park (on the right) check on the other side of the road and, tucked down in a corner below are The Tusks. They are much better approached on foot from the south, through rather a maze of streets, but locals can always point the way. If you want a map the tourist office is situated at Discovery Point, which has Dundee's proudest showpiece, Captain Scott's ship *Discovery*.

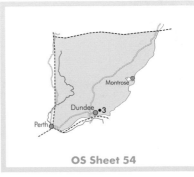

OS Sheet 54

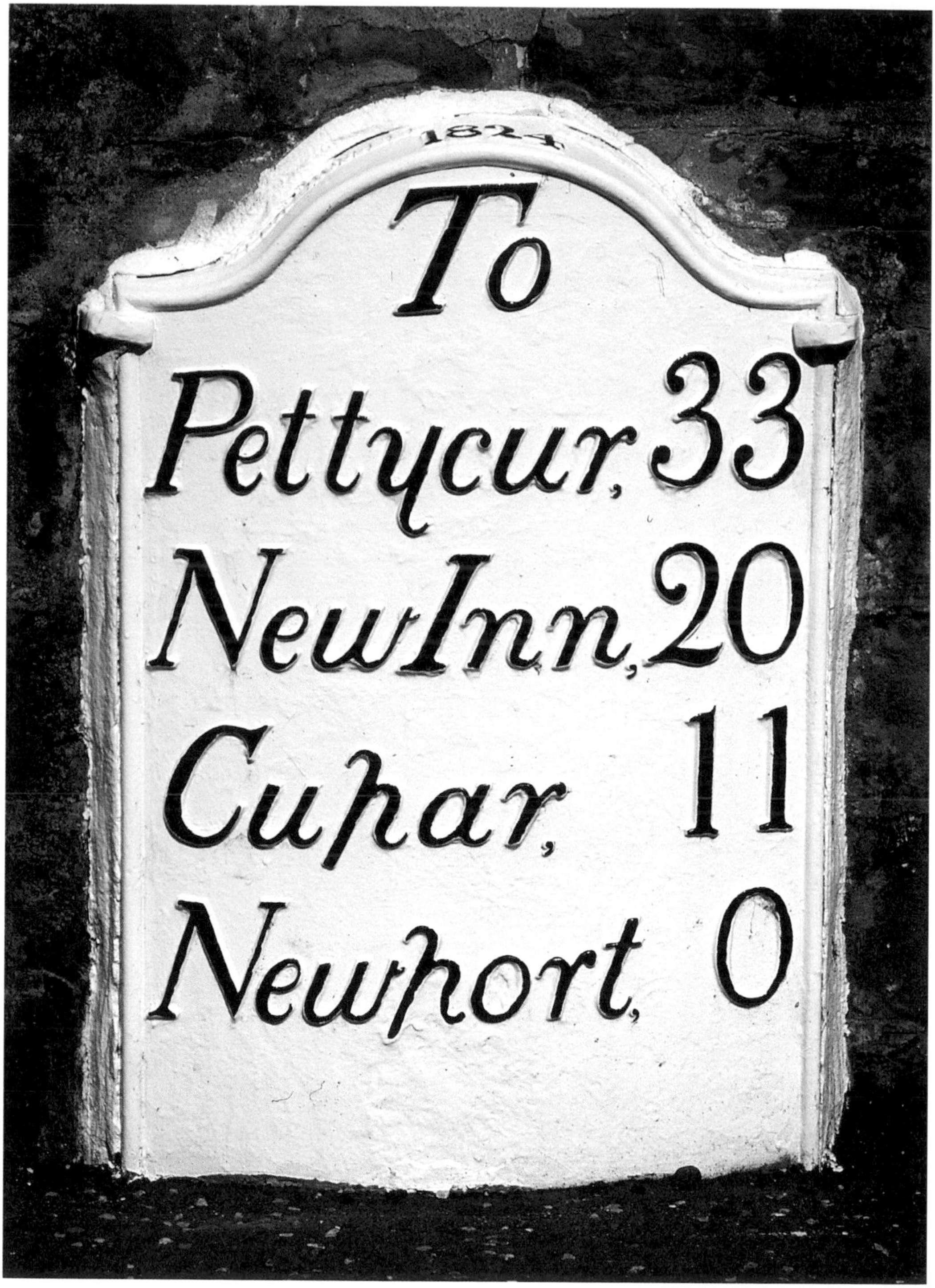
1824
To
Pettycur, 33
New Inn, 20
Cupar, 11
Newport, 0

1
ZERO MILES

'Pettycur 35' miles on a milestone may puzzle but points to the small harbour arm below Kinghorn on the Forth looking across to Edinburgh. At one time this was the major crossing point for traffic from the capital heading to St Andrews, Dundee or Aberdeen. Burntisland gave the route the death blow by ferrying people across the Forth in their railway carriages – till the mighty Forth Bridge also brought that to an end. So, crossing Fife via Cupar you came to the Tay Estuary and the crossing to Dundee and the north at Newport, another crossing which vanished with the building of bridges. In case you didn't realize you'd arrived after the shoogly coach drive across Fife the milestone makes it quite clear: Newport O.

The busy A92 across Fife and the bottleneck of Cupar takes vehicles to the bridge so leave it at the roundabout immediately before the bridge and drive west to reach the site of the old ferry. The milestone is set by the wall on the left, facing the one time ferry buildings.

East fife has an unusual variety of milestones, and a suprising number of them so, driving anywhere, keep an eye open for these. Some are very precise; you may see for instance, Anstruther 3⅝.

OS 59: 418278

2

KATE KENNEDY

Kate Kennedy was the niece of Bishop Kennedy the founder of St Salvator's college which would grow into the well-known University of St Andrews. Kate is a shadowy figure who, however, is the centrepiece of a pageant that is held in the spring each year. This involves portraying all the historical figures connected with St Andrews and, each year, one male, *bejant* (first year student) is always chosen to be Kate. The whole is organised by the Kate Kennedy Club, an ancient institute which was revived in 1926 and, WW2 apart, has promoted the procession round the streets of St Andrews ever since – over 60 years without a break.

In few other places were/are 'town and gown' so closely connected and the number parading runs into three figures – quite a collection of costumes to maintain. And carriages. Kate rides with her uncle and attendants amid piles of daffodils while Archbishop Sharp is dragged from his carriage and murdered several times along the route.

A barefoot St Andrew comes out from the pend at St Salvator's Chapel to lead the procession while a commentator indicates just who is who, rather a lot of saints, monks and prelates to start with, including the notorious Cardinal Beaton who was hung from a window of the castle for his sins. There are the poor reformers who were burnt in the town: Paul Craw, Patrick Hamilton and George Wishart, those who weren't burnt: John Knox, George Buchanan, Andrew Melville. Plenty of Kings and Queens, inevitably including Mary Queen of Scots – and her love-worn French courtier, Pierre de Chastelard, who, found under her bed for a second time, had his head chopped off. Covenanting days parade Samuel Rutherford and Alexander Henderson (both buried in the Cathedral graveyard) and the resplendent 'Great Marquis' Montrose who was a St Andrews student (and golfer, – as was M Q of S). There are figures from the Jacobite risings and a succession of Rectors including Earl Haig, John Stuart Mill, J M Barrie, Kipling, Nansen, Frank Muir and John Cleese, the last doing his 'walk' of course. There are quite a few goodie Victorians who brought the town and university out of the doldrums, founders of this and that, a student who made an astonishing rescue to a wrecked ship, a newspaper reporter with his white terrier trotting along beside him.

Having friends in St Andrews I've usually been warned not far in advance when the Kate Kennedy will happen but trying to pin it down proves difficult. Perhaps the best bet is to check periodically with the Tourist Office: tel. 01334-472 021. Perseverance will be well rewarded. The picture opposite shows the 2001 Kate.

OS Sheet 59

3

BUCKIE HOOSE

A 1692 house in Anstruther Wester was taken over in mid C19 by 'an agreeable eccentric' as Robert Louis Stevenson called him. The slater covered the walls with patterns of seashells, everything from large scallops and razor shells to whelks, topshells and winkles. Shells in Fife are simply referred to as *buckies* so the house soon became called the Buckie Hoose. The slater, Alexander Batchelor, also covered the walls and ceiling of a room inside – and his ready-made coffin.

He advertised: 'This is the splendid grotto room / The like's not seen in any toon. / All ye who do wish it to see, / It's only 3d asked as a fee', then added '(And a 1d to lie in the coffin)' – which Sandy was quite happy to do. After Batchelor's death in 1866 he was duly buried in his shell-covered coffin. The Buckie House fell into disrepair and was nearly demolished in the destructive Sixties but the NTS had it restored and occupied in 1971. In 2010 it was brought into pristine condition once more thanks to local enthusiasts.

Others of a similar nature have all disappeared in my lifetime, including a garden in Leven which even had a bus completely covered in shells. On the other hand I have seen a new buckie hoose at Hamnavoe in Shetland.

Anstruther lies in the East Neuk on the Fife Coast between Crail and Pittenweem. The Dreel Burn runs through the town, hence Anstruther Wester, once very much a separate burgh. The Buckie House is right on the bad corner near the Dreel Burn and parking nearby not possible. So use car parks and walk. At low tide stepping stones cross the Dreel Burn on the sands. Buckie House faces the Old West Kirk, which is now used as a hall. There is a Shell House (among other whims) in the grounds of Newhailes House, Musselburgh, just east of Edinburgh (NTS).

OS59: 654035

SCOTLAND'S VIA FERRATA

Pegs and wires were strung across mountain faces in Italy during WW1 to make for the faster movement of troops; regions that saw some grim fighting. Now these routes have been re-established as a recreational thrill but we don't need to go to the Alps to find the nearest *via ferrata*.

Kincraig Point thrusts cliffs and caves out into the Forth Estuary at the eastern end of the vast Largo Bay, with Earlsferry/Elie just beyond. The Fife Coastal Path goes over the top of viewpoint Kincraig Point, 63m, with some fine remains of WW2 gun emplacements and a marvellous succession of flowers in spring, from pastel cowslips to vivid cranesbill. The Chain Walk works round below the cliffs. Created in 1929 this involves dangling across cliffs on chains, sometimes above the sea, with strenuous ascents and descents; not practical at high tide. An hour at least is needed to complete the route. In many places bucket steps have been cut, but weathering has made some of these precarious, and the rock is greasy when wet. There are no escape routes. Treat this fun passage seriously; unique entertainment, Britain's only *via ferrata* till one was recently erected on the Honister slate mine on Fleetwith Pike in the Lake District. The Chain Walk however is free and unregulated.

Out by the Chain Walk and back over the top makes for a superb outing, perhaps best done from the Earlsferry/Elie end as Shell Bay at the other end is not so easy to reach and has a huge caravan park. There are some strange features along the Chain Walk, most notably an area of columnar basalt pillars and the strange weathering on the shore below them but I'll not describe the passage in detail; much of the fun is wondering what will come next.

There is a fuller description (W-E) given as an appendix in my book *Exploring the Fife Coastal Path* (Mercat Press) 2006. There is parking at the Kincraig end of Elie/Earlsferry (one runs into the other) beside the golf course. Be early to ensure space! A path leads down to the shore through the golf course. Dogs should not be taken on the Chain Walk unless they can abseil.

OS59: 465997

THE KIRK THAT FLITTED

Churches don't often move from one town to another, the actual physical stone and mortar of the building that is, so here is one that did. I became aware of St. Andrew's Church long ago as it stood across from the school where I was teaching. The minister's wife also taught in the school and on one occasion kindly took one of my pupils over to the manse. The boy had collected a range of flowers in the hills south of Loch Laggan and there were some I could not name which she, as a botanist, might. As they sat in the manse looking up books I wonder if she was aware of the irony of the situation. The boy had been put on probation – for pinching lead off the church roof.

The church originally stood in North Street in St Andrews, designed by William Burn (1824) and with a facade added in 1853 by Sir Gilbert Scott, so an illustrious start. (It lay between St Salvator's College and the Younger Hall, looking at the street today.) Practicalities saw it put up for sale in 1870 and an expanding congregation in Buckhaven bought it – for £130. It was then carefully dismantled and taken from St Andrews harbour to the one at Buckhaven by the vessel *Sea King*. In 1872 it was again in use in its new site and does not seem to have minded changing from Episcopal to Free Church. In 1879 the storm that caused the Tay Bridge disaster blew down the cross atop the front of the church; a finial replaced it. When the Free Church amalgamated with the Church of Scotland it became the church hall and, as part of local renewal, was more recently converted into a theatre and youth centre.

Buckhaven lies on the Fife coast of the Forth Estuary just outside the Methil/Leven conglomeration and about 13km along the A955 from Kirkcaldy. The church/theatre stands at the crossroads in the centre of the town. Once quite a holiday resort, a weaving town, fishing harbour and with several coal mines in the area the town suffered severe architectural vandalism in the 1960s when most of these activities had disappeared.

OS 59: 358980

6

MONSTER IRIS

Just imagine iris sprouting up to six metres high. Approaching Glenrothes from Leslie on the A911 there is a big roundabout, the Fettykil Fox, Leslie, Roundabout – and there they are on the verge, big, bright, in natural colours. They were originally 'grown' for the memorable Glasgow Flower Festival in 1988, the work of Malcolm Robertson.

From the same roundabout the B969 southbound for south and west Glenrothes and Kinglassie soon crosses the dell of the River Leven by a striking modern bridge. To see this properly, from the roundabout continue along the A911 for Glenrothes centre and, c.350m on, turn right into Riverside Park (signposted, OS 59: 265016) and walk up to see the shining wonder. (OS 59: 261016). There are many woodland paths to enjoy walks in the Riverside Park, which continues on the other side of the A911, reached by an underpass

OS 59: 263019

COAL FURNITURE

The Kirkcaldy Museum and Art Gallery has an odd display that usually sets tongues wagging: furniture made of coal; a table, two chairs, and a dressing table mirror, all in such shiny black that many presume them to be ebony. They are 'parrot coal' to be precise, a hard type of coal without splitting planes which allows it to be carved and polished to look like this. Unlike a carpenter's work there are no joints, pins or other bits and pieces used to combine various parts. These are sculpted.

They are the work of Thomas Williamson (1817-1860) from West Wemyss and were made from local coal in 1855 for Rear Admiral James Erskine Wemyss of Wemyss Castle. (He probably owned the mine.) The chairs bear the crest of Wemyss swan and motto *Je pense*. One can imagine how they would appeal to Victorians. Prince Albert bought a seat for Osborne House and it was on show at the Great Exhibition of 1851. There is a parrot coal gravestone at St Adrian's church, West Wemyss; now moved inside to preserve it, and the red church building on the main road through East Wemyss has an exterior wall plaque with the Church of Scotland symbol of the Burning Bush carved in coal.

The Museum also has a coal tortoise, partly (the shell is natural but blackened) made by Allan Stewart. The Shop has what appear to be smaller items made of coal but they are made using a modern mix of coal and resin and are moulded, not carved. The museum has many other interesting displays, and exhibitions upstairs are changed several times a year so, graced also by a tempting café, it is not surprising that this is one of Fife's top visitor attractions. Everything is closed for a mjor refurbishment, reopening in 2013.

The Museum and Art Gallery were presented to the town by John Nairn, linoleum manufacturer, who lost his son in World War One, and they form part of Kirkcaldy's memorial garden. The war memorial itself lists a shocking number of names to be coming from just one area. The railway station lies just behind (on the road to it a VR letterbox), the bus station is near and the venue is well signposted for motorists.

OS59: 275 916

8
EARTHSHIP FIFE

Fancy a home largely built from old tyres? Earthship Fife is an example of a self-sustaining eco-friendly building and, as the illustration shows, you don't really notice the tyres though they play a major part in the construction.

Sunk into the slope, the walls of tyres, cans and other disposable fillings give the house an equable temperature so little heating is required and that comes from solar panels. Power also comes from a wind generator and running water. 'Grey water' is used in a contained system to deal with sewage, the south-facing windows also capture heat. Nothing is wasted. The building really heats and cools itself. Fascinating.

The setting is a delight, overlooking Kinghorn Loch, with a whole range of examples of sustainable developments, woodland walks, bird hide, etc. Kids love it. The site is at Craigencalt off the A921 Fife coast road; from the west take the B923 from Burntisland's second roundabout, from the east turn off right onto the B923 just as Kinghorn is reached. Signposted thereafter. Guided tours, recycling projects and demonstrations take place and local volunteers and the disadvantaged are encouraged to work on site. Details/brochure from Sustainable Communities Initiatives, Tel: 01592-891884. Website: www.sci-scotland.org.uk

OS66: 258875

1

LIGHTHOUSE AS MONUMENT

Perched above the Sound of Mull not far from the eye-catching Duart Castle this remains one of Mull's oddest memorials: a lighthouse raised to the memory of William Black, a name that won't set many bells ringing.

William Black (1841-98) was a once popular author of romantic adventures whose books are almost unknown today. As a boy I read one or two but they hardly measured up to G A Henty or R L S. You can sense the sentimentality in titles like *A Princess of Thule, A Daughter of Heth* or *Macleod of Dare* – this last set in Mull (which the author had visited), the island painted as a pretty dismal place for the London actress brought here by the hero. The memorial however is worth a visit for the setting is romantic enough. Oddly the light is half-way down the steep slopes and not on the cliff top.

The light was built in 1900, the money subscribed by friends, with the proviso that the architect had to be William Leiper (designer of Templeton's Carpet Factory, see p.119). The Lighthouse Commissioners agreed to these odd arrangements. The dark tower is stark with a higher conically-capped stair tower alongside; the whole effect could have come out of one of the novels.

The coast can be followed for the kilometre south from Duart Castle or, parking carefully half a kilometre before the castle, a way made across fields, rough walking and coastal crags – the memorial is tucked away below them. Duart Castle, home to the Macleod chief, should not be missed of course – and it has a good tearoom.

OS 49: 753343

2
CAIRN WITH A VIEW

One of the finest views I know and have visited several times has a commemorative cairn just below the summit. It perches a kilometre off the A82 as the road climbs up onto Rannoch Moor from Loch Tulla, on the NW shoulder of the 492 hill, Beinn Mhor (height but not named on the map). It can clearly be seen from the A82 heading south as the road drops to the lochs. There's a view all round: over the Moor, endless hills, into the heart of Coire Ba and down to Loch Tulla.

The cairn is well-built and has the inscription:

IN MEMORY OF / RONALD HARVEY / WHO DIED DEC 1 1962 / AGED 26

WE CAST HIS ASHES TO ROAM

ON THE WINDS, OVER THESE HILLS

WHICH HE KNEW, LOVED AND ROVED SO MUCH.

WE LEAVE HIM TO TRAVEL ALONE

THE PATHS WE TREKKED TOGETHER.

HE SHALL BE WITH US WHEN WE RETURN.

THE ROAR OF THE STAG

THE CRY OF THE BIRD

THE SIGH OF THE WIND

SHALL BE HIS CONSTANT COMPANIONS.

HIS PASSING / HAS BEEN THE SUNSET OF OUR FRIENDSHIP

Ronald Harvey was killed nearby on the way home after a day on the hill. Friends and family built the cairn and have looked after it over the years but only two are alive today and no longer able to get on the hill.

There is a layby for parking near the Rannoch Rowan (the landmark tree growing out of a boulder) and a track as far as small masts.

OS 50: 302472

3

ST CONAN'S KIRK, LOCH AWE

This has to be one of the oddest churches anywhere yet the building is also stunningly effective. Every feature of ecclesiastical architecture has been incorporated and the unorthodox result should have been a disaster; instead we are given endless surprises and may even laugh outright at some touches while the view from the chancel through the arches of the ambulatory is unforgettably beautiful. So many designers would have used stained glass but, here, the clear glass gives a view of woods and hills and lochs which, as some Benedicite tablets elsewhere declare 'all praise the Lord'. So how did this messy part-abbey or pseudo-cathedral come to be set by the shores of Loch Awe? Looking timeless St Conan's dedication was, surprisingly, in 1930.

The coming of the Victorian railway saw the nearby hotel built and various mansions erected, including one on the island, Innis Chonain for Walter Campbell, brother of Lord Blythswood. Folklore has it that his mother found the carriage drive to Dalmally Church wearisome so he built the church 'next door'. This was a simple affair, built between 1881 and 1886, but in 1907 he started on the grander vision. He was his own architect, woodcarver and collector of oddities – like the bone of Robert the Bruce on display. (The effigy was by Alexander Carrick who sculpted the figure of William Wallace at the entrance to Edinburgh Castle and Bruce had a memorable skirmish in the Pass of Brander not far from St Conan's.) The work was entirely local, the granite stone not quarried but trundled down off the slopes of Beinn a' Bhuirdh above. Campbell died in 1914 when work was suspended anyway. After the war his sister continued working to his plans and when she died in 1927 the Trustees completed the complex.

I'm not going to over-describe St Conan's; the joy of a visit is its serendipity nature but don't fail to wander out or round to the far terraces above the loch. Saxon tower, flying buttresses, the entertaining dog chasing hares gargoyles, St Conan himself (also by Carrick) all set the scene. Inside, use one of the guidebooks available to explore or you'll miss oddities like the oak beams recycled from the battleships *Caledonia* and *Duke of Wellington*, remains of mort safes, the Skerryvore bell, the fishing boat font and all the stories of where certain features came from to be incorporated here.

St Conan's lies on the Loch Awe side of the A85 in the straggle of Lochawe village. The Carrick war memorial (a kilted soldier) at the entrance is a good landmark. Coming from the east drive on a bit to a lay-by: steps lead down to the church. Coming from the west there's a lay-by opposite the entrance. Disabled can park at the entrance, circled by a pseudo stone circle.

OS 50: 116267

4

CHOLERA GRAVE AT ARDNOE POINT

Ardnoe Point offers a walk for the adventurous. Crinan itself is hardly quick to reach, the northern end of the Crinan Canal, linking Loch Fyne with the Hebrides. However, as you approach Crinan the important thing is to take the road down to 'Crinan Harbour' for the start of the walk to the point. A car park is indicated and the start of the walk co-incides with a set piece, waymarked round described on a board in the car park: green posts with a symbol of a puffer (ship). This wends along the shore then through the woods and then turns uphill.

Where it does so a small path heads off right (just before a green post) and this is the way to Ardnoe Point. Rough, jungly, slaistery, true aqueous Argyll so, if you don't like the first stretch, give up. The way wends in and out, up and down, over streams, bogs and clawing vegetation all the way for about half an hour. The round-topped gravestone sits under a large ash tree and could easily be missed when the bracken is high so a visit would be best in spring when the primroses are in flower, the bracken still has to unfurl, and the midges haven't acquired their blood lust.

The story of why we have come is inscribed on the stone: 'Erected by Isabella Estoh in memory of her husband John Black, Feuar and Fish Cliver of Greenock, who died of cholera on his schooner *Diana* and is buried here, 28th July 1832, aged 45 years'. At that time infectious diseases like cholera could neither be prevented nor cured and were rightly feared. A harbour would probably have been denied to the *Diana*.

Some of the flat rocks on the shore hereabouts are scoured with passing ice from past Ice Ages, striations clear. Bits of shore might prove more congenial for the return journey. Do take in the canal locks road end before leaving the area: always interesting and there's a very welcome coffee house. The whole region hereabouts has the heaviest concentration of prehistoric sites in Scotland.

Since visiting Ardnoe I've come on a more accessible monument to another cholera victim, a John McLean who died in August 1854 on board ship and was buried close to the shore west of Lochranza in Arran. (OS 69: 918508)

OS60: 918508

5

A ROUND CHURCH

This church would be strange almost anywhere but on Islay somehow looks remarkably at home, dominating the view looking up Bowmore's wide purpose-planned street. White and clean-gleaming it stands in a walled graveyard, the church dating to 1767, the kirkyard walled in 1775. It was built by Thomas Spalding for the Islay laird Daniel Campbell of Shawfield who may have brought the idea or plans of a circular building back from his recent European Grand Tour. Italy and Jerusalem had round churches though far more complex and decorated than this white-harled drum with its conical cap of dark slate. A tall central wooden pillar supports the roof. One C18 stone records a family tragedy at sea with the depiction of a sailing ship but what I found especially sad, in an added corner, were the rows of wartime sailors' graves, so many bearing the wording 'Known Unto God'.

The ferry service to Port Ellen (from Kennacraig – West Loch Tarbert) and then local bus to Bowmore is the easiest approach, the road between straight for mile after mile as it goes across a great bog. On the edge of it lies the island's airport. Tourist Information Centre, The Square, Bowmore, Tel: 08707-200617. The name Bowmore is also well known for its distillery – down the hill – and Islay malts are famous. The peat has one good use. Note Islay is pronounced *Isle-ah*.

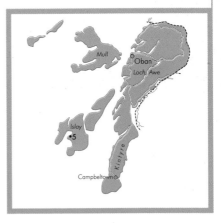

6

DAVAAR ISLAND'S CAVE 'CRUCIFIXION'

Davaar Island (116m) sits dumpily at the entrance to Campbeltown Loch and is safely reached three hours each side of low tide by a long spit of gravel and sand, the Doirlinn. A 1754 lighthouse lies at the lower north end of Davaar while below the higher, craggier south end is what is known as MacKinnon's Cave. In the cave is the interesting painting of Christ on the Cross which was 'discovered' in the summer of 1887.

A yachting party came on the figure, somewhat naïve but more appealing than subsequent efforts. There were soon crowds crossing to view the wonder, thousands eventually in the first weeks. The speculations can be imagined (some declared it 'miraculous') but when the local school's art teacher Alexander MacKinnon was found to be the artist he soon found himself done down in true Scottish fashion, even accused of using the school's paints. What he had done was give a very real boost to Campbeltown's economy which continues to this day. But he shook the mud of Argyll from his feet, eventually settling in Nantwich in Cheshire.

In 1902 MacKinnon returned to Campbeltown to restore the painting and in 1934, aged 84, the town council invited him back again. The version this time was more sophisticated but rather sentimental. Now he was a local hero. At the ceremonial completion both Church of Scotland minister and Catholic priest attended, an ecumenicalism rare at the time. A year later MacKinnon died.

Head of art teachers have kept up the tradition since World War Two, touching up or changing details a bit over the years. The Community Council paid for another restoration in the 1970s and so it remained till 2006 when a vandal stenciled Che Guevara's face over that of Christ. Ronald Tognieri, who had done the work in the Seventies, did so again, hopefully with materials that will last better – and reward the many visitors who still find Davaar fascinating, despite the plastic tat left by some.

There are other caves and sheep and goats graze the uninhabited island. Its porphyry stone built the houses and streets of the town. The tourist office displays the vital tidal information.

Drive through Campbeltown, along past the harbour, residential area and tanker pier, to a lay-by where a gate leads to the shore and the start of the Doirlinn. Be shod adequately. On Davaar work round right and the painting is in the fourth cave, on the left wall. Too difficult for me to photograph I've done a sketch. Campbeltown Tourist Office, tel: 01586-552056. An interesting book *Curiosities of Argyll* by Marian Pallister (Birlinn) has three versions of the painting illustrated.

OS 68: 760191

REST AND BE THANKFUL

I first came to know this road during cycle trips as a boy, on one occasion even going up by the original road which wends below the razor slash of the A83 through Glen Croe. I've also had to pedal *down* the five miles of glen against a fierce headwind. Pity then the poor redcoats who constructed the old road, one of Caulfeild's, in the aftermath of Culloden. It wended along all too near the valley bottom so to mount the headwall had to put in some hairpin bends. I can recall car rally enthusiasts tackling the climb and have read of older cars only coping with the final demands by going up in reverse gear.

Now there's a big car park on the summit, from which there is a fine gun barrel view down Glen Croe, Beinn Luibhean and the Cobbler on the left, Ben Donich and The Brack on the right and with Beinn an Lochain behind, towering over Loch Restil. In 1743 it was decided to build a road from Dumbarton to Inverary (the seat of the pro-government Duke of Argyll) but the 'Forty Five' rising meant it was 1748 before troops could be spared to work on the road: the 24th, later South Wales Borderers. The route was completed in 1749. In 1768 the 93rd, Sutherland Highlanders, repaired the summit stretch and left the stone with some of the details and the words 'Rest and Be Thankful' on it – which can still be seen at the far end of the top level parking area. In 1814 the military roads were transferred to the Commission for Highland Roads and Bridges, the body which wisely appointed Telford as chief engineer.

In 1818 the poet John Keats and a friend, Charles Brown, set off on a walking tour, starting at Lancaster and taking in the Lake District, Galloway, the Burns Country, Loch Lomond, across Mull for Staffa and Iona and from Oban to Inverness, with an ascent of Ben Nevis thrown in. They set off from Loch Lomondside for some hours of walking, planning to breakfast at what they took to be an inn called 'Rest and Be Thankful'. (The first inn proved to be at Cairndow.) Dr Johnson and Boswell, the Wordsworths, Thomas Pennant, Sarah Murray, Faujas St Fond were some other early travellers who left descriptions of the pass.

OS 56: 229 073

THE DENNY TANK

A friend called this "one of the oddest things I've ever seen". The tank, as long as a football pitch was built for testing models of proposed ships and was built in 1882. It holds 1.75 million litres of water. There are plenty of other interests in the museum as well. Outside sits what could pass as a modern sculpture: the engine from Robert Napier's 1824 paddle steamer *Leven* which was built in Dumbarton. (Denny's great clipper ship *Cutty Sark* was also Dumbarton built.) The building itself (A-listed) has a polychromatic façade, the sort of swank work taken to extremes in Templeton's Carpet Factory, p.119.

Dumbarton lies on the Clyde between Glasgow and Helensburgh. If travelling from the city take the A82. The Stirling-Loch Lomond A811 also gives easy access. The museum is well signposted when entering Dumbarton and was refurbished in 2010. There is a small café. Oh, and you can try your hand making a hull model and testing it in a mini tank, something which appeals to children of all ages, many of them adult. Open: Mon-Sat 10-4. Tel. 01389-763444.

The Scottish Maritime Museum has three sites, the major one at *Irvine* on the Ayrshire coast (tel. 01294-278283) and *Clydebuilt, Braehead,* off the M8, Glasgow-Erskine Bridge road, south of the River Clyde (tel. 0141-886-1013). All are fascinating and have plenty of hands-on activities, but the *Denny Tank* is certainly one of the oddest things to see.

A CRANE CALLED TITAN

The name of John Brown's shipyard is forever recalled because of 'the Queens', the liners *Queen Mary* and *Queen Elizabeth* (and don't forget warships like the *Vanguard*) and the closing of the yard was something of a national blow as well as a local tragedy – as if Clydebank had not suffered enough in the wartime blitz. One reminder of those days survives and has been turned into an extraordinary visitor feature – the crane they call Titan.

This massive structure towers over 45m high and it is no surprise to find the engineer who built it was Sir William Arrol, best known for his work on the Forth Bridge. It was built at Dalmarnock and erected in 1907 and the cantilevered arm is capable of lifting 800 tons and is an A-listed 'building'. Now painted a delicate blue the crane still dominates the area but, beside the view *to it*, now one can enjoy the view *from it*, from on top. The white tower beside it is a lift in case you were worrying. Enjoy the ride. You will be amazed once up to the jib platform and wheelhouse. Digital wizardry lets visitors see the launching of the Queens!

The site is well signposted on the south side of the A814 Glasgow-Dumbarton road. (On the north side lies the Clyde Shopping Centre and the Forth & Clyde canal.) Head down Cart Street and past the Clydebank College to the Purser's Office. All visits are made from there by a courtesy bus. You can of course walk along the waterside and look at it across the old fitting out basin – but not gain access. From the centre of Glasgow trains run to Clydebank Station and buses to Clydebank Bus Station and are only a 15 minute walk from the site. Plenty of car parking space.

Open: May-October, Friday-Monday, 10.00-17.00. Tel: 0141-952 3771.

OS 64: 495 697

GOT NO BALLS

If one walks up Port Dundas Road, not far after crossing Cowcaddens Road, Buchanan House, built as British Rail's Scottish HQ, lies on the right – a five minute walk north from the Glasgow Royal Concert Hall or the city's main bus station. In front of this is a striking-enough sculpture, called 'Locomotion', the naked sprinting figure inside the hula-hoops which are representing the 'power and virility' of railway travel. There is a double irony perhaps, both on the man's virility and the present state of our railways: the figure of the man has been given no genitals! Were we that prudish in 1967, Frank Cossell?

Actually we were. I did a programme about birds with some pupils for the BBC that year and in the conversation one of the boys mentioned the way Victorian prudery had given one poor bird the quite meaningless name 'wheatear' to replace the accurate Anglo Saxon 'white arse'. It was cut.

5
ON GLASGOW GREEN

Glasgow Green was given to the people as a common in the C15 and was the most famous recreational and meeting place for the east of the city. It was a drying green into the C20. There are many interesting and unusual features on its green acres by the River Clyde but I'll just describe three, each marvellously odd in some way.

The People's Palace

Glasgow's People's Palace is a huge glass-domed, rufous Dumfries-shire sandstone structure, a rather typical C19 swanky municipal gesture. Opened in 1898 it is a mix of museum and winter garden and there is nothing like it in Scotland. Where else would you see a Single End, eight huge Ken Currie murals, an Anderson shelter, displays on Crime and the Bevvy, along with Billy Connolly's big banana boots, all under one roof? But the museum sets out to show working class life as it was, reflecting the struggles, strikes, marches and demonstrations of the past two centuries many occurring on The Green. Many of the everyday items came from the demolition of central Glasgow.

The building itself was the palatial work of the city engineer, A B McDonald and the figures of Progress, Science, Mathematics, Engineering, Art et al were by Kellock Brown. The astounding Winter Garden is a huge steel held glass dome (four times the size of the museum) which has the garden features *and* space for concerts or other activities and an excellent café.

Doulton Fountain

This faces the People's Palace and is the world's largest such made of terracotta, gifted to the City of Glasgow from the Doulton Company for the Glasgow Exhibition of 1888. It was moved here in 1890. Four years later lightning destroyed the statue of Queen Victoria. Henry Doulton provided a replacement. The fountain was designed by A E Pearce and was modelled by the students of Lambeth School of Art under W S Frith. The ornate and complex work was nearly lost; neglected, no longer spouting and many of the figures taken into storage. The £15 million

Glasgow Green Renewal project saved it. The statues (water-bearers, soldiers, a sailor, figures for Canada, India, Australia and South Africa) portrayed the 'glory of the colonies and dominions of the British Empire' and there's a nice irony in the fountain now flowing in all its glory outside the most democratic of museums with the Empire 'aw weed awa'.

Templeton's Carpet Factory

This is at the east end of Glasgow Green and is visible from the Doulton fountain. On the

way you may pass one of the city's most-loved sculptures, set in the garden beside the palace: a boy playing pipes to enchanted squirrels at his feet. It's the work of Thomas Clapperton. Locals, wrongly, refer to it as Peter Pan. You can see why. On from it lies the one-time carpet factory.

The Doges' Palace in Glasgow sounds a bit unlikely and even odder is the fact that the building which draws that comparison was a carpet factory. I used to pass it regularly in the years before all the demolitions and motorways and I rather assumed it had disappeared. Accidentally coming on the building recently I let out such a squawk of surprise and delight that several people turned and looked at me. Well, it's that sort of place. If you don't believe me, here are two descriptions I've recently read or heard: 'It is quite simply spectacular, mediaeval Italian architecture carried far beyond anything the Guelphs or the Ghibellines could aspire to, with a polychromatic façade beggaring description', or, more succinctly, 'It's way out man!'

The town council had been turning down J & J Templeton's plans for a factory and almost in despair they employed William Leiper to design a building of unimaginable style that would finally satisfy the fussy city fathers. (Leiper was asked what he considered the most spectacular building he knew of and mentioned the Doges' Palace.) Red sandstone, red terracotta, Ruabon brick, vitreous enamel mosaics in rainbow hues, glazed bricks, in every complex combination, make it like nowhere else. And behind this facade lay a working carpet factory. In 1889 the façade, insufficiently tied back, collapsed and killed 29 weavers.

They simply rebuilt the collapsed front, complete by 1892, added to the factory in the thirties then it fell under threat after WW2. Mercifully, in 1980-85 was saved and converted to a Business Centre. The original Templeton, James, started as a draper but began carpet manufacturing in 1843, moving to Glasgow Green in 1856 and handing over to sons John and James in 1878.

OS Sheet 64

Glasgow Green can be reached by buses 16, 18, 40, 61, 62, 64, 203, 263 from the city centre. Free car parking nearby. The People's Palace is open daily, 10.00-17.00 (11.00 on Friday, Sunday). Tel. 0141-271 2951.

AN ITALIAN P.O.W. CHAPEL

Ah Orkney? Well, no.

This is a story which I only discovered following the re-opening of Glasgow's Kelvingrove Art Gallery and Museum in 2007. There are surprising similarities to the Orkney story but this P.O.W. camp was in Lafaruk in what was then Somaliland. Something like 40,000 prisoners were cooped up in that desert wilderness and, as in Orkney, they yearned for a chapel – so they also built one, out of mud bricks and scrap. They too had a resident artist who painted a charming triptych with a Madonna (Regina pacio) flanked by worshiping angels, the camp seen in the background. It was painted by using flour bags as the canvas.

Unfortunately, at the end of WW2, Somali soldiers (there to keep order!) rampaged through the camp and smashed the chapel and badly damaged the alterpiece. The prisoners managed to rescue the paintings which were passed to the British commanding officer, Cpt. Alfred Hawsworth, and brought back with him to the UK. He had fully supported the Italians in building the church and had done his best for the prisoners generally. He kept in touch with the artist, Giuseppe Baldan, and the families visited each other over the years. In time Hawsworth suggested the paintings should return to Italian keeping but they would not hear of this. They declared they owed their very lives to their old C.O. and wanted the works to stay in Scotland so the alterpiece was eventually donated to Kelvingrove by Mrs Hawsworth. 'You must keep them for ever as a gauge of gratitude and love by the 35,000 people who owe you , beyond their lives, the dignity of a humane treatment.' A nice touch in the paintings has the camp laundry fluttering in red, white and green – the colours of the Italian flag.

The paintings are simple – and beautiful – and are given a quiet corner so you can sit and hear the story I've given briefly and also read other details available. They are not easy to find so ask at the desk in the main hall. And if visiting Kelvingrove allow plenty of time, it is a rich cornucopia of a place. Good cafes and restaurants too. Parking in the area is not too difficult and buses from the city centre pass the main entrance. Glasgow Tourist Information Centre: 0141 204 4400; Kelvingrove: 0141 287 2700.

OS Sheet 64

THE GREENOCK CUT

Interesting in itself this feature also offers one of the most scenic walks in Scotland. The cut is simply a water channel cut to feed Greenock with badly-needed water in the C19, both for drinking and for industry. (James Watt was born in Greenock.) Engineer Robert Thom was given the job which deserves the accolade brilliant rather than odd. He created a whole series of reservoirs including the largest, now named after him, from which the cut made a 6.5km circuit to a pond high above Greenock and then ran down in two flows, each turning many mill wheels in their descents. Another 5km Kelly Cut tapped the Kelly Burn above Wemyss Bay. Wooden mills, paper mills, foundries, shipbuilding, sugar refining all flourished – and health was much improved. The cut was built in 1825-1827. One of the risks was there being too much water following excessively wet spells, so sluices run off the surplus, a purely mechanical yet automatic system of great ingenuity which you can see explained, with much else, at the Cornalees Visitor Centre.

Cornalees lies besides the Compensation Reservoir below Loch Thom's dam and has a really superb display, tearoom and information on walking the cut, a circular route of 10.5km. Sluices, bothies (where men lived who broke up the ice in the cut in winter), the varied wildlife, flowers, the almost level path are then topped by the views. Working anti-clockwise are the Gare Loch, Loch Long, Holy Loch, Dunoon and the Cowal Peninsula, Bute, the Cumbraes and the peaks of Arran. Wow!

From Greenock take the B788 Kilmacolm road to start but when it turns left (traffic lights) keep on up the hill on the B7054 'scenic route' to Largs. Turn left opposite Overton Primary School onto the Old Largs Road and twist up to pass a golf course and so to Loch Thom with the Cornalees Visitor Centre. A small road also heads up from the A78 a couple of kilometres NE of Inverkip – or from Largs. If unable to make a long walk you can still get much of the flavour from a very short walk at the Greenock end. Heading up as described, instead of turning onto the Old Largs Road keep on up Drumfrochar Road then left onto Overton Road to a car park. A footpath angles up to the cut from which the views soon open out.

The cut can be walked anytime. The Cornalees Visitor Centre is open daily, Apr-Oct 11.00-16.00, in Nov-March only at weekends 11.00-15.00. Tel. 01475-521 458.

OS 63: 246 721

CASTLE GRAFFITI

This must be one of the oddest sights in Scotland. Having seen a picture of it I decided it just must be included in this selection. What I found was a great deal more. The castle itself is Kelburn Castle, home of the Boyle family, Earls of Glasgow who have developed a Country Centre like no other. I have never seen so many happily engaged children.

The brilliant graffiti on the castle can be viewed across the deep and attractive Kell Burn *den* or from close up – if you can get children past the falconer with a barn owl on her wrist, the indoor play-barn, pony riding, a wild west stockade, pets' corner, adventure course and the secret forest. But this buzz is equally easily left behind for splendid walks in forest and glen, for 50 year old Wellingtonias and 1000 year old yews, Monterey pine and unique weeping larch (Heritage Trees), a formal walled garden and panoramic views over the Clyde to Arran, Bute and the Cumbraes. There are a lot of unusual touches and adults will also be happily engaged.

Kelburn Castle and Country Centre lies a few miles south of Largs on the Ayrshire coast (A78). Open: Apr-Oct, 10.00-18.00. Grounds year round, in winter 11.00-dusk. Tel. 01475-568 685. The graffiti may not be a permanent feature so check beforehand. Historic Scotland had only given temporary permission for this extraordinary treatment of an historic castle.

OS 63: 216 565

THE INVENTORS' BRIDGE

The River Garnock and the River Irvine join and thereafter reach the sea through a channel which has an unusual bridge for pedestrians – it can retract one side to make an opening for yachts and anything high to pass through. The name comes from having a metal screen running along its length on which are the names of famous Scottish-born inventors: Watt, Murdock (not Murdoch), Telford, Black, Simpson, Symington, *et al*.

The bridge led across to The Big Idea, a grassed-over dome, a millennium facility a bit like the Glasgow Science Museum, which has since closed. The bridge is at present shut though retracted a couple of times a week to keep it functional and one can still see it – and the names – from close up.

Walk upstream and you'll come on the popular local-history sculpture of The Carter and His Horse, a life-size work by David Annand. A puffer and other vessels of the Maritime Museum (housed in huge sheds nearby) are a bit sorry looking and one can only hope the area revives in the future.

OS 70: 304381

MURDER ON GOATFELL

At the small graveyard at Sannox on the east side of Arran there's a railed-off boulder inscribed 'In loving memory of Edwin Rose, who died on Goatfell, 15 July 1889'. Nothing odd in this, except Edwin Rose, a 32 year old Brixton builder's clerk had been murdered on the mountain, the only known such case. (Fiona Graham, whose name is given to the listed 2000-foot Scottish hills, was murdered in Kintail in 1993 but not *on* the hill). Rose was seen on the summit of Goatfell on a Monday with a companion Annandale, both of them having mixed with others over the weekend. On the Tuesday their landlady found they had gone and simply shrugged off her loss of rent. Only when Rose failed to appear off the London train being met by his brother was there any concern shown.

There was a week of searching before Rose's hidden body was found, the head and face 'smashed' and left shoulder fractured, his belongings strangely scattered on the slope above, (his hat, folded in four, held down by a stone). Annandale also skipped Rothesay digs without paying and returned to work but was questioned by a fellow worker who'd seen him on Arran with Rose. Annandale, real name, John Laurie, promptly sold his tools and vanished. He wrote odd letters to newspapers from Liverpool and, returning to Scotland, was caught leaving a station near Hamilton.

The jury took forty minutes to return a verdict of 'Guilty, by a majority': 8 voting 'guilty', 7 voting 'not proven'. Nobody voted 'Not Guilty'. Laurie/Annandale died in Perth Criminal Asylum in 1930. The odd thing however is the absence of all direct evidence that he committed the murder. Everything was circumstantial. The verdict was no doubt correct but for wrong reasons. Today's forensics would surely have shown him guilty.

An odd footnote. At the trial the Arran police were unhappy answering questions about what had happened to Rose's boots. Only by persistent questioning did it come out that they had been buried on the beach, with the Chief Constable present. It was believed in Arran – even in 1889 – that a murdered man's ghost would walk again unless his boots were so buried.

OS 69: 015 453

BURRY MAN

This strange figure can be met with in Queensferry on the second Friday in August each year. Covered in burrs from head to foot, crowned with flowers and with flowery staves, the Burry Man parades through the town lying on the south of the River Forth between the two great bridges. The superstitious rite must have its origin in past pagan millennia though there are suggestions it reflects the idea of the scapegoat for, at the end, outside the town, the burdock burr skin is peeled off and burned – as if the sins of the town had been cleansed for another year. Similar festivals took place in Fraserburgh and Buckie at one time and lingered on in Eastern Europe. Queensferry now seems to be unique and there, the ritual is kept going largely through the dedication of local enthusiasts.

I was lucky to see the preparations one year. A green flannel suit is first put on and then prepared sections of the locally-collected burrs are stuck on. A balaclava is donned and in the end only eyes peer out from a figure encased in burrs. Garlanded and with his staves (and two supporters) he sets off round the town, a bell-ringer before and children chanting set words behind, a considerable ordeal on a hot day and with generous refreshments offered *en route*.

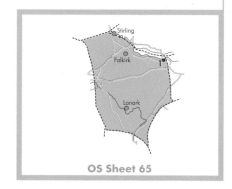

OS Sheet 65

2

SCOTTISH KOREAN WAR MEMORIAL

This stands in a quiet yet accessible spot in the Bathgate hills at the SW corner of Beecraigs Country Park. Opened in 2000, the 50th anniversary of the start of the Korean War, it commemorates, and lists the names of all British servicemen lost in that four year conflict – which involved forces from 21 UN countries.

A wooden pagoda with a red tiled roof holds the names of the fallen, the shrine set in a tree-studded pattern of yin and yang (the symbol on the Korean flag). Throughout the ground 1090 birch trees have been planted, one for each British fatality, 88% of whom were National Servicemen aged eighteen and nineteen.

From the west end of Linlithgow's High Street turn up Preston Road (signposted for Beecraigs Country Park) climb steadily out of the town, crossing the Union Canal, and then twisting up into the hills. At a junction (Beecraigs to the left) continue along the Bathgate road.

Shortly after entering the trees there's a small car park hidden in the wood off right. A path from there leads (in about ten minutes) to the 278m top of Cockleroy which has been described as the finest viewpoint in Lowland Scotland. Continuing on the Bathgate road; the trees cease on the right and are thinner on the left. Keep a careful watch, left, to spot the surprisingly eastern temple-like building of the memorial and park in a lay-by immediately after. Enter by the wrought iron thistle gates.

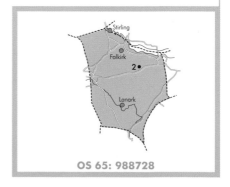

OS 65: 988728

THE PINEAPPLE

The Pineapple is a folly of magnificent swank, towering over the buildings, gardens and trees of the Dunmore Estate near Airth, not far from the Kincardine Bridge. From a range of buildings rises a Gothic tower with high windows and on top of this soars the pineapple, accurate in every detail and the detail is impressive: every jutting leaf curve for instance has its own drain to prevent frost damage and chimneys are disguised as ornamental urns. Facing south, down the grassy expanse from which visitors generally see the wonder is a classical loggia entry, on the north side a Gothic doorway leads in to the second storey. The pineapple alone is 16m high. It doesn't so much look like a pineapple; it is one. The keystone above the south entrance bears the date 1761 which would make the Pineapple the work of John Murray, 4th Earl of Dunmore who'd succeeded to the title in 1756.

Above this south entry there's a marriage lintel style heart and motto 'Fidelis in Adversis' which commemorates the marriage of George, 5th Earl to a daughter of the Duke of Hamilton in 1803. He bought the island of Harris in 1834. Amhuinnsuidhe Castle was built there by the 7th Earl (who explored Spitsbergen, Arctic Russia, Hudson Bay, Kashmir and Tibet) and in 2005 saw a much publicised community buy-out.

Why a pineapple? For sheer swank of course but very much of its time when such an exotic tropical fruit would only appear – and rarely – on the tables of aristocrats. I've seen a pineapple carved onto gravestones (Kirkcaldy Auld Kirk) which could well have been connected with a merchant trading to the Indies and, after all, the 4th Earl of Dunmore was Governor of New York and Virginia and then of the Bahamas. Out there it was a practice, to indicate one was at home and welcoming visitors, to leave a pineapple on the doorstep. Building one in stone was a zany idea but one man's folly becomes all men's pleasure. The name of the architect is not known.

The Landmark Trust has the building on a long lease from the National Trust for Scotland and has restored it for holiday letting, but it can still be viewed in all its glory across the southern park and a return to the car park made through the woods. There's a pond, home to great crested newts, rarest of Britain's newts. No toilet facilities. At the complex interchange south of the Kincardine Bridge take the A905 for Stirling, passing through Airth and about 1km on the site is signposted, left. Another kilometer along the A905, right, is the attractive village of Dunmore, which was laid out as a planned village, and worth a visit. The blacksmith's has a horseshoe-shaped doorway.

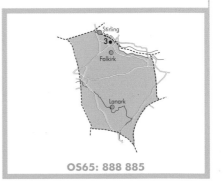

OS65: 888 885

4

RADICAL PEND, BONNYBRIDGE

A pend is simply a passage, in this case under the Forth & Clyde canal at Bonnybridge, built to allow workers, carts and the like to get to and from work. (The bridge over the canal came later.) The pend has a yellowy stream coming out of it so there's a raised walkway for pedestrians. A note on the arched entrance reads 'The Radical Pend. Named to commemorate the Battle of Bonnymuir. April, 5th 1820'. Battle it never was but a cruel suppression against an industrial demonstration. Hard working conditions and a depression following the Napoleonic Wars led to demands for universal suffrage and other parliamentary reforms. Terrified of a repetition of the French Revolution the government suppressed demonstrations brutally, as in the 1819 Peterloo Massacre in Manchester. Here, some 300 Calton (Glasgow) weavers got caught up in a march to Falkirk and were set upon by mounted troops. Three demonstrators were executed for sedition and others transported.

It is hard to envisage Bonnybridge as once a sprawl of industrial works, much situated by the canal, the last of which only vanished in my lifetime. From the canal walk down the brae and turn right at the Mill Garage where you will spot the pend.

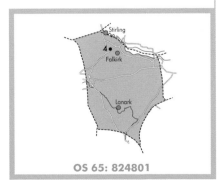

OS 65: 824801

THE TRIG POINT MONUMENT

Major General William Roy (1726-90) was known as 'the father of the Ordnance Survey' so it is happily odd that the monument near Carluke marking his birthplace is in the shape of the familiar trig point (trigonometrical pillar). His father was factor of the Hallercraig estate. In 1747 Roy was appointed to extend Wade's work surveying in the Highlands. He worked on fortifications but his special skills lay in mapping, especially in the south of England with the ever-present threat of France. He fought at the Battle of Minden. He was made Surveyor General in 1765 and in 1783, from a Hounslow baseline, organised the triangulation from London to Dover (to link with Paris) and then radiating out, reaching Scotland in 1809. A keen antiquarian, FRS, he comes over as very much an Enlightenment figure. He died just as the great survey was to start and his monument, on site, is two cannons upended to mark the two ends of his base line. One now sits between two semis on Roy Grove in Twickenham Borough and the other is located in a corner of a long-stay car park at Heathrow airport. Scotland has done much better.

From the Lanark, south, end of Carluke (A73) at a grassy area backed by a modern housing estate turn west onto Cartland Avenue. The turning is signposted 'General Roy Monument', and simply follow the signs. Once onto the 'no through' road look out for the sign, right, for Gillbank. The monument is immediately on the right past this crossroads, 2.7km from the A73 and marks the site of Miltonhead, his birthplace.

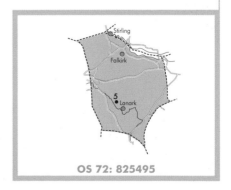

OS 72: 825495

ONE O'CLOCK GUN

In central Edinburgh it is easy to tell visitors from locals at one o'clock in the afternoon: visitors jump, locals look at their watches. The One O'Clock Gun has just been fired from the castle – as it has been every day (except Sundays) since 1861.

The observant standing on the battlements might see a simultaneous time signal given over at Calton Hill where there is a tower in memory of Nelson, built in 1807, looking like an upended telescope, with a mast on top. Since 1853, on nearing the hour a ball is taken to the top of the mast and, synchronised with the castle and the Greenwich time signal, drops at exactly one o'clock. This gave ships at Leith or in the Forth the chance to set their chronometers accurately, essential then for accurate navigation. When the gun was first synchronised with the time-ball a 4000 ft (1219m) cable linked them, laid by sailors in just two days. Some of the original mechanisms are in the Huntly House Museum. The gun was brought into use because smoke or fog could often obscure Calton Hill; Edinburgh was called Auld Reekie after all.

The gun used for many years was a 25-pounder, now a 105mm light gun fires the time signal from the north-facing Mill's Mount Battery. Visitors can watch Sgt Shannon ('Shannon the Cannon') of the 105 Regiment, Royal Artillery perform his daily task. Previously he was in charge of firing the giant five ton Mons Meg (forged in 1449) to bring in the New Year. If visiting Edinburgh Castle allow yourself plenty of time; there is much to see.

2

DOWN THE HIGH STREET OF EDINBURGH

Starting at the Castle the Royal Mile runs down to Holyrood Palace, the initial stretch, Castlehill soon becoming the Lawnmarket and only then the High Street. Don't try and combine this walk with visiting Edinburgh Castle; the Castle needs several hours and should take in one o'clock – see p.141. The Esplanade is actually the property of Nova Scotia some maintain. When James VI made his barons of Nova Scotia, a money-raising ploy, technically it could only be done on Nova Scotia soil so the Esplanade was declared to be part of Nova Scotia. Our walk is highly selective, noting a few oddities rather than the many famous buildings or associated people.

Cannonball House

Setting off, the gable on the first house, right (facing down the Esplanade), is generally referred to as Cannonball House from the obvious iron ball lodged in the stonework but a few metres to the right is another – shattered – ball so the name really should be in the plural. Nobody knows why they are there. Folklore has it they were fired from Edinburgh Castle during the Forty Five. Another theory suggested the ball marked the gravitational height of the first water supply. Just over on the other side of the Esplanade is the Witches Well which marks the spot where scores of women were burned to death in the years 1479-1722. There's a rather odd inscription.

Heading down Castlehill, on the left is the Camera Obscura (whose white dome is well seen from the Esplanade) then, right, the one-time Tolbooth Kirk with its 73m steeple, the city's highest. Walk down on the right side, now the Lawnmarket, and watch out for Brodie's Close.

Deacon Brodie

William Brodie was known to the citizens of C18 Edinburgh as the upright Deacon of the Guild of Wrights, those who worked in wood. However in 1786 he used his skills to forge keys (taking putty or clay impressions) and then employed them for what we call breaking and entering: super-respectable by day, a thief in the night. Then cupidity became stupidity: he robbed the Excise Office and fled to Amsterdam. He was extradited and hanged at the Tolbooth – on a gallows of his own designing!

Continue down, cross the North Bridge (the toga-clad figure across the High Street is David Hume – who deserved better) and you come on a highly ornate memorial.

The Duke of Buccleuch Memorial

This is to the 5th Duke of Buccleuch who was also the 7th Duke of Queensberry (1806-1884). He inherited a galaxy of titles and great acres and mansions at the age of thirteen. Three years later he would act as host at his Dalkeith House for the visit of George IV and was called upon to do the same in 1842 for Victoria and Albert who considered Holyrood Palace not up to standard. Largely ignoring law or politics the duke is simply remembered as someone with a wide range of interests, dedicated efforts and philanthropy. (He built Granton Harbour at his own expense.) I think the memorial reflects how he was viewed. At first glance it looks just like another aristocratic figure on a pedestal. But look closely. You may smile and I'll not spoil expectation by saying why.

The Heart of Midlothian

Beside the memorial to the duke once stood the old tolbooth, the Heart of Midlothian. The tolbooth was stormed in 1736 during the Porteous Riots and demolished in 1817. Small brass rectangular markers pick out its outline in the causey stanes (Scotland's setts/ rectangular cobbles) and in the middle of these is a *Heart*.

In years past you would notice the Heart as people would always swerve round the mark, stepping on it being considered very bad luck. As a boy I'd be quite worried seeing anyone do so but now people stream along and most never even notice it. Several people have also mentioned the habit, which I've not seen, of people spitting on the Heart for luck. Jeanie Deans, the heroine of Scott's novel *The Heart of Midlothian* is mentioned on p.173.

We are more or less at the main entrance to St Giles High Kirk (or Cathedral in Sassenach terms), of considerable interest, the Thistle Chapel one of its wonders. For now, going round to the right of the building, one reaches Parliament Square – which also has the cathedral's excellent café entrance, a good place to end.

FLORAL CLOCKWORK

Edinburgh's Floral Clock, created in 1903, by the Parks Superintendent John McHattie, was the world's first and, judging by the crowds at it every summer, remains one of the best. Each year a different anniversary is commemorated and in spring athletic garden staff sprawl on ladders across the steep slope to plant the 25,000 or more annuals and succulents to create the appropriate display. Even the hands of the clock are planted. The Carrara marble statue of C18 poet Allan Ramsay with his silk nightcap stands aloof above the colourful display with the clock's mechanism in the pedestal. The works for the clock originally came from the clock tower of Elie parish church; recycling 1903 style, but have been replaced twice since.

Princes Street Gardens, so attractive now, was the site of the old Nor' Loch, a stagnant lake usefully guarding the Old Town but was drained (late C18) with the creation of the New Town. Gardens for houses along Princes Street were safeguarded by an Act of Parliament in 1827. Commerce took over the street but the gardens have flourished despite the coming of the railway, the Gothic extravaganza of the Scott monument and a couple of Greek Temples set in the middle! At one time it was proposed that the Union Canal should run through the gardens and down to Leith. Princes Street is still regarded as one of the world's most evocative streets and few visitors will fail to see the year's floral clock.

The clock lies, through a gate, just below the street level of Princes Street, on the west side of the Mound, the road running up past the Greek Temples (which house the Scottish Royal Academy and the National Gallery of Scotland).

Some of the anniversaries I recall: the Territorial Army's centenary (illustrated; 2008), the centenary of the Scouts, the 50th year of the Duke of Edinburgh Award, the Queen's Golden Jubilee, the 50th anniversary of Enable Scotland, 200 years since the birth of Hans Christian Anderson and the 500th since the founding of the Royal College of Surgeons – quite an eclectic list.

CRAIGENTINNY MARBLES

This tongue-in-cheek name is well-deserved for one of Edinburgh's most notable yet least known oddities which is simply a mausoleum, though there is nothing simple about it. The architect was David Rhind. Suburbia has overrun the area but the Christie Miller Mausoleum still dominates the surrounding bungalows – it is big, very big. The *Buildings of Scotland* describes it rather well: "A huge segmental pedimented Roman mausoleum shocking the prim houses surrounding it".

Miller was the late son of a wealthy merchant (who only married when 91) and, though an MP, was something of a recluse whose characteristics had his sexuality questioned. (Was 'he' a 'she'?) Speculations would never be answered for when he died in 1849 he was buried 20 or 40 feet down (architectural guides vary), below solid rock or concrete, and with the towering mausoleum over his remains. People were left with their prurient speculations. He was nicknamed 'Measure Miller' owing to a habit of measuring all the books he bought, a rule being carried for this purpose. He retired to the family mansion of Craigentinny House in Restalrig Village as it was then.

Towering up, like some Greek temple in scale, is the far from simple mausoleum, in grey sandstone, but the two larger sides with intricate marble relief depictions of 'The overthrow of Pharaoh' and 'The Song of Moses and Miriam', by the sculptor Alfred Gatley. They are rather splendid.

The Craigentinny Marbles lie on Craigentinny Crescent, off the major Portobello Road, left, descending. Bus routes 5 and 26 descend Portobello Road and, if motoring, there is no problem parking. The extraoridnary Piershill pets cemetery is on the right, immediately before Craigentinny Crescent when descending Portobello Raod.

OS66: 290744

GOLDIE'S WILL; WRIT IN STONE

The Rev James Goldie died in 1847 'the last of his race' and the stumpy obelisk over his grave bears weird details of his *will*. Very difficult to make out the wording but it declares 'Bequest to the General Assembly's Education Scheme £100; to the Indian Mission £100; and the residue of his estate amounting to £4000 sterling to the Royal Infirmary of Edinburgh under burden of a perpetual annuity of £5 to be given by the minister and kirk session to the poor of the parish of Temple on Christmas Day'. Isabella Goldie, on the reverse has something similar, some words illegible, then 'the interest of which to be given also to the poor of the parish on Christmas Day'. As there are no poor in Temple today – and no church either – one wonders what went with the £4000, a huge sum in 1847 – over £230,000 today.

This old (C14) Midlothian church, the only surviving Templar building in Scotland, in ruins now, was replaced by a new one just across the road and it is now a private house. Temple is best found by going south down the A7 from Edinburgh. At Gorebridge (which is just off the A7) a sign on the right indicates Temple 2, Penicuik 10. Along this B6372 the observant will spot (right) the attractive 'Cougar Gates' of the Arniston estate. There's a junction, left, for Temple then, almost at once, turn right and descend a brae to the old church. There are several interesting grave stones in the kirkyard, one, right next to the Goldie obelisk, outstanding: a farmer (John Craig, d.1742) stands in his C18 Sunday best with his two young boys at his sides, his hand resting on the head of the elder.

OS 66: 313 587

Opposite: The obelisk with the inscribed wills and, right, the fine C18 famer's stone.

A ROYAL CONVENIENCE

Finding a public toilet with a royal insignia on it was something of a surprise. There is a crown and the royal cipher of George V (1935). In 1935, however, it had this mark because it was opening as a GPO telephone exchange. The change of use only came in the 1960s so we are left with what signs at Holyrood Palace call a 'lavatory'. Dalkeith's indicates 'Toilets'. There is also a notice which should not be taken too literally: 'Ladies, Disabled and Baby changing room' (Just you try changing my wife!)

The A68 off Edinburgh's ringroad bypasses Dalkeith so follow the town signs off it and park where possible in the town centre; usually not too difficult. The toilet block (signposted) is a bit hidden but lies just off the High Street – a High Street first noted back in C13 (Tolbooth is 1648) but Dalkeith's greatest showpiece is the splendid House (Palace).

This lies at the NE corner of the town, a Country Park setting with much of interest. The main castle-into-house building was done by James Smith in the C17 (who also did the vanished Hamilton Palace) but was added to by William Adam and William Burn and it was here the Duke of Buccleuch entertained George IV on his visit (1822) and Victoria, as queen, first put foot on Scottish soil. There's a tea room in the Adam stable block which also has 'conveniences', whatever they are called.

OS Sheet 66

A TOTEM POLE IN PRESTONGRANGE

Having come on this totem pole in the barony of Prestongrange (Prestonpans) I then have met others in Scotland including one at Inverie in Knoydart, but this is by far the biggest and grandest, erected in 2006 to celebrate Prestonpans' thousand years. It is made of red cedar which came from British Columbia but every inch is carved and painted and decorated with details from the town's history. (The oddest item is an inserted brick.) The whole idea took complex community efforts on both sides of the Atlantic and is detailed on a plaque.

This Scottish-Canadian connection also led to the establishment of a Murals Trail and there are twenty six murals, all nearby, with historical details pictured. Details are given at the totem pole and leaflets are available to guide visitors round the very varied artworks.

There's parking (seaward side) beside the totem pole while across the road is the Goth, a popular pub/restaurant. The odd name is a shortening of Gothenburg, pointing back to historical trading between the countries. (Page 3 tells of a Gothenburg ship coming to grief.)

Coming from the Edinburgh-Musselburgh direction follow the coast road. The totem pole is seen, left, shortly after reaching Prestonpans. Coming from the east the huge Cockenzie power station is passed just before reaching Prestonpans.

Edinburgh
7 Haddington

OS 66: 381742

OPPOSITE: The brick mentioned is below the teapot

THE COW IN THE TOWER

A few miles north of Haddington in East Lothian a tower rises on the top of the Garleton Hills; a few miles west of Cupar in Fife a tower rises from the top of Mount Hill. Both are named Hopetoun Monument. They are reputedly intervisible, they are both commemorating Sir John Hope who took command after the death of Sir John Moore at Corunna and brought the Peninsula War to a successful conclusion. He'd become the Fourth Earl of Hopetoun on the death of his half brother.

Mount Hill, alas, has been largely covered in conifers and the tower is not open but the East Lothian monument is both open and easy to reach and is worth climbing for the view which many reckon the very best encompassing the Forth estuary. And the tower has a tale.

Cows are remarkably able climbers given the chance and on one occasion a cow went into the tower and started upwards. Realising this was not a good thing it tried to turn but couldn't. Cows are not good at reversing so panic set in with the inevitable explosions of bowels and bladder. Lurching and sliding and bellowing her head off (the noise might have been noticed in Fife), two farm hands came to the cow's rescue. The only thing they could do was to push the brute back – once they managed past the cork-in-bottle bulk. That proved a difficult and dirty task and so did the hour of labour following. Bull-running had nothing on cow wrestling. At last one cow and two farm hands tumbled out the door, all three exhausted and green from hair to toe and horn to hoof. A sign was put up: 'Please shut the door'.

The A6137 from Haddington to Aberlady runs west of the Garleton Hills and the B1343 off it circles the north of the tower. As the hill is reached, there is a small car park, right, from which a path climbs up through trees to the open summit. The tower may be ascended. (Please shut the door.) The Mount Hill Monument in Fife lies off the Cupar-Newburgh A913 (OS 59: 334165).

OS 66: 500764

RECYCLING IN EYEMOUTH

In the High Street of Eyemouth is a cemetery which is unusual in having the gravestones all replaced against the perimeter wall. In the centre stands the monument to the Black Friday tragedy of 1881 when 189 fishermen from this coast died in a sudden storm.

But there is really oddity on oddity here: the original cemetery became full, partly from the demands following a cholera outbreak so, about 1849, the stones were removed and soil added, to a depth of eight feet or more, to allow burials to continue. Some of the displaced stones were used to build the watch house in the corner. The stones are very obvious but many, being soft sandstone, have weathered badly. Newer stones tended to be granite. And in 1881 they in turn were moved to the surrounding wall and the 'broken mast' monument erected.

Eyemouth was, and is, the largest and best protected of the Berwickshire fishing harbours, at the mouth of the Eye Water. The museum in the old church has a fifteen feet wide tapestry to the 1881 disaster, created for the centenary and should not be missed. Nearby the statue of Willie Spears is to one of the leading fishermen who fought against the legal impositions of the time.

OS 67: 944644

1
HUNDY MUNDY

This must be one of the oddest names appearing on a Scottish OS map in that rolling landscape north of the River Tweed between St Boswells and Kelso. Hundy Mundy is a folly pure and simple, built as an eye-catcher for the great house of Mellerstain two miles to the NW. From there it occupies a skyline gap in a row of mature trees. The work is attributed to William Adam (d.1748) the founder of the famous family of architects. Mellerstain is a huge Georgian sprawl, home to the Earls of Haddington. The 12th Earl was an amateur jockey (he won the Grand National in 1933) and owned a horse he called Hundy Mundy.

The folly takes the form of an arch, flanked by pepper pot towers and is best seen by approaching from the west, from the B6397 which leaves the A6089 shortly after leaving Kelso. Drive through Smailholm and at the first crossroads turn right onto a minor road which angles about the Mellerstain policies. As you begin to climb Hundy Mundy comes into view, outlined against the sky between the trees – how it should be seen. At a bend a motorable track leads off to a parking area at the end of the wood. At the track's start you can pick up a leaflet explaining the present use of the wood. Some might regard this as odd, or natural, and I'll leave you to discover and decide! There are wide and attractive views, away to the distant Cheviots and, of course, to Mellerstain House. A kilometre on leads back to the A6089.

On such odd names hereabouts, at Duns Castle Country Park a lake in the grounds has the name Hen Poo – also on the OS map. (OS 74: 778546)

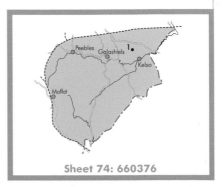

Sheet 74: 660376

2

DOLLS AT SMAILHOLM

Smailholm Tower is just how a Borders' peel tower is imagined: a stark fort perched on a rock commanding wide views over the countryside. The tower can be seen from ships approaching Berwick. The tower's earliest history is not known but for generations it was the home of the Pringles. David Pringle and four sons perished at Flodden in 1513 and the English attacked the tower in 1543 and 1546. The Scotts of Harden purchased the property in 1645 but they abandoned the tower for nearby Sandyknowe's greater comforts. A descendant had a 'wee sickly laddie' with polio sent to stay with them in 1773 – who would grow up to become Sir Walter Scott. J M W Turner made several paintings of Smailholm in which the toddler appeared. There Scott imbibed Borders story and fable so, not surprisingly, his first book was *The Minstrelsy of the Scottish Borders* (1802) in which much of the material was collected by Scott, Hogg, Leyden and others. His own *The Eve of St Agnes* and *Marmion* would use the Smailholm setting.

But it is not the tower, interesting though it is, that is unusual. Each floor, in turn, has display cases with what I suppose can be called dolls, but they are *big*, beautiful, and a complete surprise. They were the work of Borders' artists Anne Carrick and her husband MacDonald Scott. They illustrate characters and scenes from the ballads and legends popularized by Scott: the historical, the romantic and the supernatural in turn. Several people suggested they deserved being classed as odd, in the sub-section 'wonders': they are, and I heard one unlikely youth call them 'Dead brilliant'.

Smailholm lies NW of Kelso, in the care of Historic Scotland. Tel: 01573-460365. Open all year but check winter days which vary. Leave Kelso by the A6089 then soon turn off onto the B6397. Follow this on and up to Smailholm village. Turn left and left again at the Smailholm Tower sign. Wend on and drive carefully through Sandyknowe Farm to reach a field-edge car park with the castle perched above. Only the stark tower survives, all the other additional buildings clustered round have gone. Smailholm must be one of the most rewarding castles to visit. An odd fact: Captain Cook's father was from Smailholm Parish.

OS74: 637346

OPPOSITE: True Thomas and the Queen of Elfland

3

POETS' CORNER

The Millennium had many good spin-offs, one being this idea in Selkirk. Just along the road from the fine Mungo Park monument an eyesore building was turned into Poets' Corner by having boards covering it with dozens of poems, a mini-anthology of the Borders with Scott and Hogg, Andrew Lang and J B Selkirk, a well-quoted Anon, Tamlane etc. With the Flodden Monument visible nearby Craig's 'Dream of Flodden' and Jean Elliot's 'The Flowers of the Forest' are appropriate. I came away singing that oddest of Hogg's poem that ends, 'Up the water and o'er the lea / That's the way for Billy and me'.

At the Millennium the Scott Selkirk Group was formed and, every year since, in the first weekend in December the town dresses up and returns to celebrate the period of Sir Walter Scott. Lady Judy Steel and others of a committee choose the poems, local bodies and businesses sponsoring the project.

O! Many a shaft, at random sent,

Finds mark the archer never meant!

And many a word, at random spoken,

May soothe or wound a heart that's broken.

Sir Walter Scott

OS Sheet 73

ELGIN MARBLES

Plaster casts of significant portions of the famous Parthenon frieze plundered by the Earl of Elgin are on display in Peebles. Elgin had seen the French shipping off antiquities and decided Britain should have part of the spoil so, with the doubtful authority of the Turkish government and encouragement from our own, he set to work. What with purchasing and shipping (1803-1812) he ran up expenses of about £75,000 (many millions today) but after lengthy negotiations all he received from the miserly British government was £35,000. The originals are in the British Museum and Greece, not surprisingly, wants them back.

Quite a few museums up and down the country have casts of part or all of the frieze, now known as the Elgin Marbles. The Peebles set was acquired by the publisher-philanthropist William Chambers and it is the story behind this which makes the display both odd and astonishing.

William Chambers was born in Peebles in 1800 and moved to Edinburgh to seek his fortune. From a small bookshop he went on to publish his own topographical and biographical works, founded and edited *Chambers Journal*, much of this with his brother Robert. He became Provost of Edinburgh and very wealthy. He built a second home near Peebles and presented the town in 1859 with what was known as the Chambers Institute, housing a library, museum and gallery, the complex entered by an arch facing the High Street. The courtyard would later be graced by a war memorial which could deserve an entry on its own: an arched cupola, the dome of brilliant copper and the cross, inside, glittering with saracenic mosaics.

Head up the stairs (near right corner on entering) for the Chambers Room. This was the original Victorian museum, full of plaster casts of famous sculptures like the Dying Gladiator and the Venus de Milo, most of which were destroyed in the years of decay following World War Two. The wall friezes survived and, on entry, will stop visitors in surprise: both walls carry 18.6 metres long marble friezes, left, the Elgin Marbles, right, the work of Danish sculptor Bertil Thorvaldsen, showing the Triumph of Alexander (one of only two known), the original being carved for a palace (in just three months) for Napoleon's entry to Rome in 1812.

The restored Chambers Room was opened in 1990 by Sir David Steel MP. Explanatory leaflet on site. Open office hours. Robert Chambers was an even more prolific writer and is now best known, largely through a book which had to be published anonymously, *Vestiges of the Natural History of the Creation*, a study anticipating Darwin, which in those prejudicial times would have made him a social outcast if he'd been known as the author.

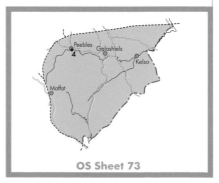

OS Sheet 73

5

THE MAPA SCOTLAND MYSTERY

This must be one of the most unusual features in Scotland yet was almost unknown until recently. An oval, sunken, walled area, 175 metres in circumference was created in a Borders landscape in which a relief map of Scotland was made, surrounded by 'sea' and rivers flowing from 50 sources. Painted like a Bartholomew's map the effect must have been astonishing, so just how did it come about and how did it drop so completely out of public knowledge? After all, the map lies just off the A703 at Eddleston, not far from Peebles, in the grounds of the Barony Castle Hotel. The OS never featured the unique site on maps though so visible from the air.

During World War Two Scotland was home base for large numbers of Polish forces. Many servicemen could not or would not go home after the war, including General Stanislaw Maczek who settled in Edinburgh. The hotel became HQ and Staff College for the Polish forces and they laid out a map of Scotland on the hotel's putting green to help with strategic planning. When the building became a hotel again after the war it was taken on by a Jan Tomasik who had served under Maczek – and married his daughter. Together they hit upon this great map as a memorial and thank you for the hospitality they had received in Scotland. Despite the Cold War a young Polish student geographer, Kazimierz Trafas, from a Cracow university, came with four colleagues to lay out the precise outline of Scotland and build the concrete map. (Maczek had seen an outdoor map of land and water when fighting in the Netherlands in 1945.) The Great Map of Scotland was completed in 1975. When Jan Tomasik died the hotel changed hands several times, served other purposes and the map fell into decay, the mechanics no longer working and the site soon overgrown – and forgotten. (The general's Edinburgh home in Arden Street is marked with a plaque. He died in 1994, aged 102 and was buried in Breda in the Netherlands.)

However, hope returns. The present owner of the Barony Castle Hotel, De Vere Venues, had the site drained and cleared of undergrowth and a campaign is now under way to raise the money for a full restoration. The map is perhaps the most extraordinary object in this volume and fascinating. For more about it and perhaps contribute, contact www.makers.org.uk/place/Maczek; email mapascotland@gmail.com. To reach the map, turn off the A703 (westwards) at Eddleston, signposted for the hotel and follow the drive to the romantic-looking castle's car parks. Head left of the hotel building and on reaching a back court turn left through a gate for steps down to the bridge over the ravine (which is a surprise too) and on the other side the map is signposted. Astonishment guaranteed.

OS 73: 235472

A MURDERED PEDLAR

Eskdalemuir is a quiet corner, hence the Tibetan monastery nearby, but it once had its very own notorious murder. Across the road from the attractive church there's a small graveyard dominated by an obelisk to a forgotten reverend. Near the SW corner is a stone covered with writing which deserves a place here. Remember the mason was probably paid by the word!

In memory of John Elliot, Pedlar, a young man of 19 years of age, who came from the neighbourhood of Hexham, in Northumberland, and travelling in company with a man of the name James Gordon, said to have come from Mayo, was barbarously murdered by him at Steel-Bush-edge on the farm of Upper Cassock, on the 14th day of Novr 1820. After the greatest exertions on the part of Sir Thomas Kilpatrick of Closeburn Bar, sheriff-depute Thirlestane, and many others, the above named James Gordon was apprehended at Nairn, and brought to Dumfries; where, after an interesting trial he was condemned, and executed on the 6th day of June 1821. The inhabitants of Eskmuir in order to convey to future ages, their abhorrance (sic) of a crime which was attended with peculiar aggravations, and their veneration for those laws which pursue with equal solicitude, the murderer of a poor, friendless stranger, as of a Peer of the realm, have erected this stone, 1st Septr 1821.

The B709 is a very pleasant drive between Selkirk and Langholm and Eskdalemuir just a tiny hamlet. The church stands where the B723 for Lockerbie breaks off, the graveyard opposite.

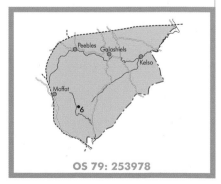

OS 79: 253978

MOFFAT'S RAM

In the middle of Moffat stands a splendid bronze statue of a ram. Known as the Colvin Fountain after the donor, William Colvin of Caigilands, in 1875, it is the work of sculptor William Brodie RSA and was intended to symbolize the importance of sheep, and wool, to the town and district. We will leave observers to decide whether it has ears or not, a controversy as old as the ram. Not far along on the same street is the Star Hotel which claims to be the *narrowest* in the country.

Moffat is a favourite stopping place still for the Tweed (A701) or Ettrick (A708) run south for the Border – and even the A74 – though I suspect many stop because of the famous Sweety Shop rather than to study the ram.

OS 78: 085033

JEANIE DEANS

Jeanie Deans was a character in Scott's *The Heart of Midlothian* and was based on the real life person of Helen Walker (d.1791), whose grave is in the kirkyard of the vividly picturesque church of Kirkpatrick Irongray. Scott himself commissioned stones to be placed on the graves of some of his 'originals' and the story of Helen Walker / Jeanie Deans is inscribed on the table stone, a grave protected by ferociously spiked railings to ensure safety from grave robbers. In a sentence Helen Walker (a poor field worker) walked barefoot to London to plead with the Duke of Argyll for her sister's life (she'd been accused of murdering her own infant) and Scott, not one to pass up good 'copy', used the story in his novel. A few years ago Judy Steel (wife of Sir David, first First Minister) wrote a play based on the story which was performed at the Edinburgh Festival Fringe before touring the Borders. Jeanie Deans had a dog named Dustiefoot.

Kirkpatrick Irongray Church lies beside the Cluden Water about 6.5km NW of Dumfries in a web of country roads and the OS 84 is really needed to reach it. There is a large car park and note at the far end the beautiful sarcophagus-like stone, the top carved with animals and flowers: 'erected by the 521 men, women and children of Irongray in the Millennium year …'

OS84: 915795

RHINOS IN LINCLUDEN

Lincluden is now a northern suburb of Dumfries. Local authorities are not noted for their sense of humour so the installation of a life size rhinoceros standing on top of a suburban bus shelter is certainly odd. Fortunately, for the bus shelter, the animal was made of fibreglass, the work of Robbie Coleman, but the inspiration of local schoolchildren (in the 1980s there was an arts grant of £1,500 to improve Lincluden which has rather been cut off by the A75). Roadworks more recently necessitated removing the bus shelter but public demand saw a pseudo shelter erected in the middle of a roadside green and the rhino reinstated on top, this time with an accompanying baby, surely the 'most fun' oddity in this book. Ironically, when Burns moved to Ellisland, a few miles north of here he wrote in a letter that Dumfries had 'as much idea of a Rhinoceros as of a poet'.

Taking the A75 round the north side of Dumfries turn off at the roundabout on the A76 Thornhill road. The rhinos will be seen on the right almost at once. Turn off and park.

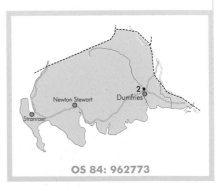

OS 84: 962773

AULD STUMPY

This is the friendly local name for Girvan's steeple. Its history has been somewhat chancy. In 1787 the town council bought ground here to serve as a market and site for a tolbooth. About 1822 a new town hall replaced the then ruinous tolbooth and the tower was added in 1825-7, to serve as a goal. (Did the bell's din come under the heading of torture?) A prisons inspector later suggested that the gaol's presence had certainly improved the town's behaviour. In 1909 the town hall was demolished and the steeple incorporated in a new hall (McMaster Hall) but this went up in flames in 1939, as did the actual spire of the steeple – which was rebuilt and given the splendid 'golden galleon' of a weathervane. So there it stands today, in splendid isolation. The barrel-vaulted cells, with latrines in the corner, still can be seen on the three floors, connected with a newel stair. A rather fine icon for the town.

Girvan lies on the south Ayrshire coast (A77) on the wide Clyde Estuary with a view out to Ailsa Craig. Sailings from Girvan are made out to Ailsa Craig – a recommended trip. Granite is still shipped from the island to make curling stones.

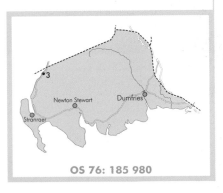

OS 76: 185 980

A UNIQUE TOWER

Hidden away in the rural world between Screel Hill (great viewpoint) and the Solway Firth is the only tower house in Scotland that was built *round*. Ochardton still has the common features of vaulted basement, an entrance on the first floor and a – very – narrow stair within the walls up to the battlements but, as a home must have been cramped and difficult to furnish. The tower would almost certainly have been the private apartments of the owners and there are attached the usual ancillary buildings: bakehouse, brewery, kitchens and probably a more spacious grand hall. John Cairns of Orchardton built the tower about 1450. Later it was bought by the Maxwells and a Sir Robert Maxwell of Orchardton was a Jacobite who was captured at Culloden. He appears in Scott's *Guy Mannering*.

To find this serendipitous gem (Historic Scotland) turn off the A711 (Dalbeattie – Kirkcudbright road) just west of Palnackie (signposted). There is a car park.

OS 84: 816552

5

CHURCH AS GARAGE

Whithorn in Galloway is a small, attractive rural town where the main interest is its historical link with St Ninian who first introduced Christianity to Scotland, long before Columba saw Iona or the Saxons of Kent converted. The site was his *Candida casa* and for centuries was an important pilgrim centre – a favourite of Robert the Bruce. There's a visitor centre and the site is open for exploration.

What caught my eye driving into the town from the north was a more recent church building (1892) which is now St John's Garage. Two pumps sit beside a booth in the doorway while a large door on the side gives access to spacious workshops, not so odd, except it must sound strange to hear a local say "I'm taking my car along to St John's for its MOT".

This comfortable conversion is on the east side of the main road towards the north end of the town. From Newton Stewart follow the A714 south to Wigtown (the 'Book Town') then the A746 to Whithorn. After Whithorn the A746 follows the coast for Stranraer; a worthwhile diversion.

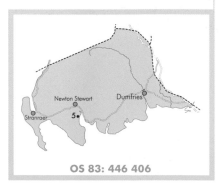

OS 83: 446 406

6

SMALLEST LIGHTHOUSE?

Gravestones can carry such a range of oddities it is difficult to be surprised but a beautiful model of a lighthouse is noteworthy – as is the setting. Kirkmaiden lies well south on the Rhinns of Galloway peninsula, that jut of land that is Scotland's extreme south west corner. The cliffbound Mull of Galloway itself is marked by a lighthouse and it was the Principal Keeper of the Light who created the model lighthouse gravestone as a monument to his son James Scott who died young, in 1852.

There are other C18 stones worth noting in this graveyard on a hill, one, much admired, in red stone, of a sailing ship. A visit to the Mull light is not to be missed; given a clear view one can see Man, Ireland, England and Wales – the mountains of Snowdonia showing over the lower bulk of the Isle of Man.

From Stranraer follow the A77, A716 and A717 south down the east coast of the peninsula to Drummore, a pretty hamlet. Heading uphill from its southern end turn right to reach Kirkmaiden. Parking is limited at the graveyard so don't block any other needed access. Logan Gardens, half a dozen miles to the north, is part of the Royal Botanic Gardens of Scotland, and worth exploring too. Because of the mild climate magnificent tropical plants survive here as nowhere else in Scotland.

OS 82: 124369

OPPOSITE: *The metre high lighthouse gravestone*

THE OLDEST POST OFFICE IN THE WORLD

This is proudly displayed above the door of the post office at Sanquhar (try *sank-er*) with the date 1763, the date from which it has enjoyed continuous use. Sanquhar was an important staging post when C18 mails were all carried by horse or horse-drawn carriages, in this case on the main route between Ayr and Dumfries – today's A76.

The post office with its distinctive bow window lies on the north side of the High Street (zebra crossing), not far from the town's fine William Adam tolbooth. The Swedish capital Stockholm opened a post office eight years later and Santiago in Chile followed in 1772. But wee Sanquhar was first.

A replica of its frontage was made by Kelloholm Workshops for the 1988 Garden Festival in Glasgow (see p.93). In the cemetery there is an inscription for an Isabella Gilmour showing she died on April 31. Robert Burns was a freeman of the burgh.

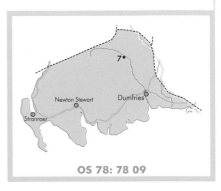

OS 78: 78 09

FOR SHEILA
*For so much over
good years.*

ACKNOWLEDGEMENTS

While most illustrations are from my own collection, held in the University of St Andrews Library, I gratefully thank the following who sourced or supplied images, the copyright of which they retain: The Clan Macpherson Museum, p.47, *the portrait of James Macpherson*; Mairi Mooney and the Trustees of the West Highland Museum, p.61, *The Secret Portrait*; Anne Burgess, p.69, *Crimond clockface*; Ken Smith, and the Stonehaven Fireblls Association, p.77, *Fireballs image*; Rev. Colin Dempster, p.79, the *St. Cryus church's curiosity*; Jane Friel and the Kirkcaldy Museum and Art Gallery, p.95, *coal furniture*; William Baxter, p.101, *the cairn with a view*; Lairich Rig, and the Scottish Maritime Museum, *The Denny Tank* p.113, Kelvingrove Museum and Art Gallery, p.121, *Italian POW altarpiece*; PSD Photography, p.153, *Prestongrange totem pole*; and the Curators of the Tweedale Museum in the Chambers Institute, Peebles, p.165, *Elgin Marbles*.

Many museums, library staff, NTC custodians, Tourist Information Centres up and down the country gave reliable help and I'm also indebted to many friends and correspondents who supplied ideas or helped on the happy exploration involved. Thank you, everyone.

One of the sources that started my interest in all things Scottish was a still precious copy of a 1974 *AA Illustrated Road Book of Scotland* with its many drawings, I frequently referred to John and Julia Keay *Collins Encyclopedia of Scotland*, the RIAS/Rutland Press *Architectural Guides* (assiduously collected as they appear), Nigel Tranter's thorough volumes of *The Queen's Scotland*, while anything to do with Covenanters is helped by Dave Love's recent *Covenanter Encyclopedia* and for older sites, all else failing, my six 1882 volumes of Groome's *Ordnance Gazetteer of Scotland* often prove most helpful. I have gleaned many ideas from the *Scots Magazine* over the years. Of more particular works I must have read hundreds in my lifetime but, recently, would recommend Ann Lindsay's *Hidden Scotland* which has some overlapping of sites and many interesting historic illustrations.

Lastly, a big thank you to Sheila Gallimore for first producing an immaculate text, to designer Heather Macpherson, Raspberryhmac Graphic Design, and to Bob Davidson of Sandstone Press for taking on the idea; a happy partnership.